WILD + FR[...]
BOOK CLUB

WILD + FREE BOOK CLUB

28 Activities to Make Books Come Alive

AINSLEY ARMENT

HarperCollins books may be purchased for educational, business, or sales promotional use. For information, please email the Special Markets Department at SPsales@harpercollins.com.

FIRST EDITION

Design adapted by Nancy Singer
from the series design by Janet Evans-Scanlon

Library of Congress Cataloging-in-Publication Data has been applied for.

ISBN 978-0-06-299821-7

21 22 23 24 25   TC   10 9 8 7 6 5 4 3 2 1

"Ah, how good it is to be among people who are reading."

—RAINER MARIA RILKE

CONTENTS

Introduction: Bringing Books to Life   ix

How to Host a Book Club   1

The Adventures of Tom Sawyer   4

Anne of Green Gables   10

Around the World in Eighty Days   16

Black Beauty   23

Charlotte's Web   29

The Crossover   36

Esperanza Rising   44

The Evolution of Calpurnia Tate   52

Mother-Daughter Book Club   58

Farmer Boy   62

From the Mixed-Up Files of Mrs. Basil E. Frankweiler   69

The Green Ember   75

Heidi   80

The Hobbit   85

Island of the Blue Dolphins   92

Falling in Love with Authors   98

The Lion, the Witch and the Wardrobe   102

Little House in the Big Woods   108

A Little Princess   114

Little Women   119

Mrs. Frisby and the Rats of NIMH   123

My Side of the Mountain   129

Collaborating with Great Authors   134

Peter Pan   138

Pippi Longstocking   145

Robin Hood   151

Roll of Thunder, Hear My Cry   155

The Secret Garden   163

The Swiss Family Robinson   169

Treasure Island   175

The Vanderbeekers of 141st Street   179

Contributors   185

About Wild + Free   193

Credits   195

INTRODUCTION

BRINGING BOOKS TO LIFE

As a child, I spent countless hours in the woods behind my house, getting lost in an imaginary world. There was a giant rock that I used to pretend was my fortress, which kept me safe from the lurking wolves and other wild animals. My parents read to me a lot, and these stories became the impetus for endless hours of imaginative play. From secret worlds to seafaring expeditions, all of my play revolved around literature.

As I got older and became less interested in adventuring, reading still remained a favorite pastime. I often took my books outside to a quiet place in the yard or even to a perch in my favorite tree. Books are their own kind of portal. Something magical happens when you read a good book, and there is nothing like getting lost in a story that makes you wish you could live there for a time.

As a bibliophile, I have a huge passion for helping kids fall in love with books and getting them hooked on literature while they're still young, so they'll come back again and again wanting more. Not every child falls in love with reading at the same age. Some do right away, but for others, it can take years. If you have a child who prefers anything and everything except reading, you are not alone. Sometimes children fall in love with experiences before they fall in love with words.

Book clubs are a great way to bring a book to life, whether your child enjoys reading or not. Children don't have to love reading to develop a love for literature. It's a gift you can bestow on them through consistent exposure and creative experiences.

When I hosted my first book club, I had no idea how much my children and their

friends would love it. We were reading *Treasure Island* and celebrated the book with adventure games in the backyard, discussion questions in the living room, and pirate snacks around the dining room table. The kids left the gathering bursting with excitement and asking when we would do it again. I overheard a few children begging their mother to finish reading the rest of the book to them when they got home.

You don't have to be an amazing organizer to host a book club. And you definitely don't need to be well read or have an English degree. The goal is to get kids and their parents reading great books together and encourage others to join you in bringing the story to life. While it takes some time, effort, and planning to get ready for a book club, it's more than worth it.

I've collected twenty-eight of my favorite book club ideas from Wild + Free mothers using some of their favorite books and activities. I hope this makes it easier for you to establish a book club so your family and friends can enjoy literature together. Among these books, arranged alphabetically by title, you'll find something for everyone. From adventure tales to animal stories, from classics to modern favorites, you're sure to find stories and activities that will delight, educate, and inspire. If you do host a book club, be sure to tag your photos #wildandfreebookclub so we can share in your experience.

AINSLEY ARMENT
Editor | @ainsl3y

HOW TO HOST A BOOK CLUB

Experiencing books through book clubs helps bring these stories to life and ensures that they stay rooted in our children's hearts for a lifetime. Although you can use the material in this book exactly as it's presented here, this book is meant to be a source of inspiration for your creativity. Feel free to adapt your gathering based on your own ideas and context. Here's how to host your own book club.

BEFORE THE GATHERING

1. Give your attendees plenty of time to read the book. Send out invitations four to six weeks before the event. Provide the details, including the book title, date, time, and location.

2. Encourage your guests to read the book before the gathering, perhaps choosing a time each day to read a chapter aloud. Children of any age can participate in reading aloud, and even the younger ones pick up on so much.

3. About a week or two before the actual gathering, send an email to the attendees with a list of food items needed so that each family can sign up to bring something. Cast the vision for the theme and invite the children to come dressed in character. I find it helpful to send a reminder email the day before the event.

4. Gather any needed supplies and invite your guests to help with the preparation. Not everyone will jump at the opportunity, but you may be surprised by their enthusiasm to help. Not only will their participation make your job easier, but preparation is more fun to do together!

5. Prepare any themed music, food, and decor to welcome attendees to the gathering. Part of the fun is helping the children feel like they are entering the world of the book. You can have your kids help you with preparing and setting up the decorations.

DURING THE GATHERING

1. As guests arrive, gather the kids in a cozy spot and start the discussion by asking them to share a favorite scene, character, or part of the book. Children are always eager to participate and share! Then ask the kids

questions about the book, starting with the simplest ones. Use the questions included here or some of your own.

2. After the book discussion, move on to the activities, crafts, and games. You can always return to the food table for more treats if you'd like, and then hand out parting gifts as the children are leaving.

VIRTUAL GATHERINGS

You could also host a virtual gathering by reading a book with friends or family members in another location and then celebrating together with online games, video chats, and even dressing up!

THE ADVENTURES OF TOM SAWYER

BY MARK TWAIN

When you read a book like *The Adventures of Tom Sawyer*, it's impossible for the images and feelings not to linger in your heart and mind for days and even years to come. A book full of stories of a child going on his own adventures is sure to spark ideas for your own kids! By giving children space to explore, discover, and live out their own adventures in an unstructured way, their imaginations can fully take flight, and they can enjoy the wonder of learning.

THE GATHERING

This is the perfect book club to host at a local park or near a creek, where the children can wade ankle-deep into the water and catch tadpoles. Nature is a portal to a whole other world of imagination and exploration. Certainly, Tom Sawyer would not have had half of the adventures he did without time spent on the river or in the cave on a secret island with Huck and Joe.

FOOD IDEAS

- Serve fried chicken or fried fish and corn on the cob.

- Make edible rafts using pretzel sticks held together with melted and cooled chocolate.

- Set up a "moonshine" lemonade stand with freshly squeezed lemonade served in mason jars tied with twine.

- Fill a few galvanized buckets with juicy apples and serve mini apple pies for dessert.

DISCUSSION QUESTIONS

1. Who are the main characters in *Tom Sawyer*?

2. Where does this story take place?

3. How does Tom avoid being whipped by Aunt Polly for hiding in the closet and eating the jam? How does Aunt Polly punish Tom for getting in late and messing up his clothes?

4. How does Tom trick his friends into helping him whitewash the fence?

5. What is Tom's reward for doing such a good job on the fence?

6. What is Jackson's Island?

7. Why isn't Tom allowed to play with Huck?

8. What kind of critter does Tom release in church?

9. Who is blamed for the murder of Dr. Robinson?

10. How does Aunt Polly find out Tom skipped school to go swimming?

11. How does Aunt Polly pull out Tom's loose tooth?

12. What does Tom do to win a Bible in Sunday school?

13. Why does Becky decide not to marry Tom?

14. What does Huck do to summon Tom outside his window late at night?

15. Why doesn't Huck go to the picnic?

16. What is going to happen to the treasure Huck and Tom find?

17. Who does Tom run into in the cave?

18. Why does Injun Joe move the treasure?

19. Who hugs Huck when they return after they were believed to be dead?

20. What is Huck most afraid of when they return to the cave?

21. How did Tom convince Huck and Joe to stay on the island?

22. Where do Tom and Huck find the treasure box?

23. Who adopts Huck at the end of the book?

24. What time of day is mentioned several times in the story and seems to be important to Tom?

25. What are some words Mark Twain uses to describe Tom Sawyer? Huck Finn? Aunt Polly?

ACTIVITIES

RAFT FLOATING CONTEST

MATERIALS

Small sticks

Hemp cord

Leaves, fabric, or paper for sails

Prizes (optional)

INSTRUCTIONS

Have the kids create a small wooden raft similar to what Tom Sawyer might have used to float down the Mississippi River. You can give them a hand, especially the little ones, but try to let them do the activity on their own. Give them about 20 minutes. After the kids have constructed their rafts, take them to a nearby creek or pool for a good old-fashioned raft derby. Prizes are optional, but lots of cheering is required!

WHITE WASHING STATION

MATERIALS

Buckets

Paintbrushes

Water

INSTRUCTIONS

Let the children "paint" a fence, wall, or any other outdoor surface with water. This will probably appeal more to a younger crowd, but it's a simple activity that children can do while you're waiting for families to arrive.

PERIOD GAMES

Play some good old-fashioned games that were popular in the late 1800s and early 1900s, like tug-of-war or potato sack races.

PARTY FAVORS

Have the children take home their hand-made rafts to keep their reading adventure afloat. Here are a few additional ideas for party favors:

- Paintbrushes and paints
- Straw hats and bandanas
- Sticks with bandanas tied to them with snacks inside to carry home
- Homemade oatmeal raisin cookies wrapped in parchment paper and twine
- Small mason jars of homemade jelly (Tom's weakness)

BY AINSLEY ARMENT

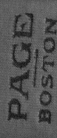

ANNE OF GREEN GABLES

BY L. M. MONTGOMERY

Reading *Anne of Green Gables* is such a delightful adventure. We get lost in Anne's vivid descriptions of the landscape and the characters she encounters. We come to love her sweet and spicy self. And yet we can easily overlook the foundational premise on which this book was written: Anne is an orphan.

Different people come into Anne's life, offering in their own unique ways the bits of mothering she needs. It's a beautiful reminder to love others around us and pour into the children we have the gift of knowing. This book teaches many lessons about what defines a family and how opening up your home and heart can change not only a child's life but also the lives of everyone that child encounters.

Let's read *Anne of Green Gables* joyously, as our imaginations delve into all of the beauty Prince Edward Island offers, while remaining mindful of the deeper foundation of this story. And let's go forth and serve one another in love, as a result of being moved by such a beautiful piece of literature. Though written over a hundred years ago, it remains relevant today.

THE GATHERING

This story can be celebrated in many different locations. A simple backyard tea party is one great idea (sometimes plain and sensible works best, as I'm sure Marilla would agree). But here are a few other locations, which give much more scope for the imagination:

- A train station
- Near a lake of shining waters
- Under the shade of a cherry tree
- An old schoolhouse
- A garden

In spite of Marilla's preference to keep things plain and sensible, feel free to add some flourishes to make *Anne of Green Gables* come to life at your book club:

- Serve tea and desserts on antique silver.
- Decorate places with lace and doilies.
- Have slates and chalk available for writing.
- Provide simple place cards and a bouquet of pink roses.

FOOD IDEAS

Here's a sample menu with items inspired by the book. The list includes quotes that you can place next to the items on the table, in the spirit of Anne's imagination and grandeur.

- **RAW CARROTS**: "Gilbert reached across the aisle, picked up the end of Anne's long red braid, held it out at arm's length, and said in a piercing whisper: 'Carrots, Carrots!' Then Anne looked at him with a vengeance!"

- **RASPBERRY CORDIAL**: "Diana poured herself out a tumblerful, looked at its bright red hue admiringly, and then sipped it daintily. 'That's awfully nice raspberry cordial, Anne,' she said."

- **ICE CREAM**: "'And we had the ice cream. Words fail me to describe that ice cream. Marilla, I assure you it was sublime.'"

- **HOT TEA**: "'I can just imagine myself sitting down at the head of the table and pouring out the tea,' said Anne, shutting her eyes ecstatically. 'And asking Diana if she takes sugar!'"

DISCUSSION QUESTIONS

1. Who do you think changes most during the novel? How and why?

2. What qualities do you think Anne looks for in a "kindred spirit"?

3. When asked her name, Anne responds, "Will you please call me Cordelia?" Why does she do this? What name would you want to be called?

4. How does Anne's character change, and how does her character change those around her?

5. Why are confessions important in *Anne of Green Gables*? Compare Anne's confessions, and discuss how each one has a different impact on her.

6. How does Marilla's character change as a result of Anne's arrival at Green Gables?

7. In what ways does Anne conform? In what ways does she remain fiercely independent?

8. When Matthew is driving Anne back to Green Gables, she asks him: "Isn't it splendid to think of all the things there are to find out about? It just makes me feel glad to be alive." Given her tragic childhood, how do you think Anne is able to maintain such a positive attitude?

9. From the moment she arrives in Avonlea, Anne insists on renaming places and inanimate things. Barry's Pond, for example, becomes "The Lake of Shining Waters,"

and Marilla's geranium becomes "Bonny." Why do you think she does this?

10. Marilla gives several reasons for finally deciding to keep Anne. What reason do you think most changed her mind?

11. "Scope for imagination" is a characteristic that Anne treasures highly in others. Discuss the role of imagination in the novel. How does it shape Anne's time at Green Gables? How does it evolve in other characters around her?

12. Good behavior is very important to Marilla and very difficult for Anne. From where do you think each derives her moral code? How do both characters change when it comes to behavior?

13. Anne is a remarkably compassionate child and is able to forgive even those who have judged her unfairly, such as Mrs. Rachel Lynde and Mrs. Barry. Why then do you think she holds such a grudge against Gilbert Blythe?

14. Why is it so important to Anne to have a dress with puffed sleeves? Why is it important to Matthew?

15. What did you enjoy most about the story?

take
home
a
chocolate

ACTIVITIES

RECITE A FAVORITE POEM

Mention this activity in the party invitation so your guests can come prepared to recite a memorized poem, or have printed copies available.

WALK THE RIDGEPOLE

Provide a balance beam of some sort and hold a competition to see who can walk the length.

NAME YOUR GERANIUM

Provide sign-making supplies so your guests can name their own geraniums. Let them take the plants home as a party favor.

PARTY FAVORS

- Vintage glass jars with chocolate chips, in honor of Matthew's gift to Anne
- Small chalkboards with colored chalk
- Teacups with bags of tea
- Geraniums

BY JENNIFER NARAKI

"'Dear old world,' she murmured, 'you are very lovely. And I am glad to be alive in you.'"

—L. M. Montgomery, *Anne of Green Gables*

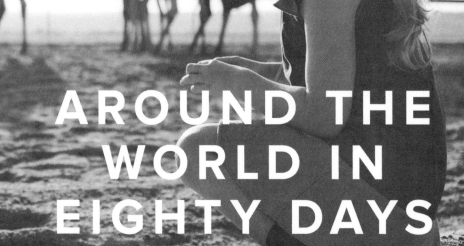

AROUND THE WORLD IN EIGHTY DAYS

BY JULES VERNE

You don't have to leave your home to take your kids on a world adventure. Try reading *Around the World in Eighty Days*.

THE GATHERING

You can gather in a home, a backyard, or a local park—anywhere with enough room to set up "stations" where you can host activities that represent the six countries included in the book. Decorate with items that represent each of the six different countries.

DISCUSSION QUESTIONS

1. Who are the main characters in the book?

2. Where does the story take place?

3. What is the name of the prestigious club to which Phileas Fogg belongs?

4. How would you describe Fogg?

5. Where is Passepartout from? Why does he often get in trouble while working for Fogg?

6. What did Fogg learn about the robber while at the Reform Club?

7. Who is the first one to suggest that it is possible to journey around the world in eighty days?

8. What support does he have for his statement? Who disagrees? What does he dare Fogg to do? How does Fogg respond?

9. How quickly does the journey begin after the bet is made?

10. How did Passepartout respond to the news that they would be traveling around the world?

11. What was the first destination of Fogg and Passepartout, and how did they get there?

12. How does Detective Fix become convinced that Fogg is the robber? Why was Fix unable to arrest Fogg when they arrived in Bombay?

13. What is a suttee?

14. Why is it decided that Aouda has to accompany Fogg to Europe? How does Passepartout get separated from Fogg and Aouda?

15. How do they travel from San Francisco to New York City, and what are some of the obstacles they face?

16. How do they end up getting back to London?

17. What happens when they arrive in Liverpool?

18. How does Fogg get out of prison? How does he make it to the Reform Club on time?

19. What does Fogg say that he won that is more important than money?

20. How do you think Fogg changes over the course of this story?

AROUND THE WORLD

This is a fun activity to help children imagine what it's like to travel around the world in eighty days. You'll set up various stations that correspond to the countries in the book, and the children will visit them with handmade passports. They will also get to try a variety of foods that represent the countries at each station. I recommend having each family sign up to bring a food item from one of the six countries. A parent will need to oversee each station to ensure that the activity goes smoothly. Suggestions are included below.

MATERIALS

Construction paper for passports

Stamps and ink from a local craft store to "stamp the passport" at each station

Any necessary supplies for the suggested activities

Food items from each country

INSTRUCTIONS

1. Make passports in advance by folding the construction paper in half, layering multiple pages, and stapling them together. You can label each page with a different country.

2. Set up a separate station for each of the six countries the kids will visit (England, Egypt, India, China, Japan, and the USA). You can set up these stations inside or outside, depending on the weather.

3. After everyone has arrived, tell the children they are about to embark on a race around the world. Depending on how many kids there are, you might decide to make it a trip around the world, instead of a race, so they can travel together.

4. Give each child a passport to take with them. Explain that they will have to travel to each country, participate in that country's activity, and try the food dish prepared for them. The parent at each station will facilitate the activities and then stamp the child's passport when they have completed their country's activity and meal.

ENGLAND: THE ROYAL GUARD

Explain that the Royal Guard is made up of soldiers who stand outside Buckingham Palace in London, England. They stand motionless and will not flinch unless you do something wrong. Tourists make a game out of trying to get these soldiers to react. Have a few kids line up and pretend to be soldiers in the Royal Guard. Have the other kids try to make them crack a smile or laugh, then have the children switch places.

FOOD IDEAS

- Fish and chips
- Shepherd's pie
- Yorkshire pudding
- Tea and biscuits

EGYPT: HUMAN PYRAMID OR MAKE A MUMMY

MATERIALS

Toilet paper (optional)

INSTRUCTIONS

Have at least five children build a human pyramid, but let them figure out how to make it work. Or assign partners and have them turn each other into mummies using a roll of toilet paper.

FOOD IDEAS

- Dates
- Baba ghanoush
- Falafel

INDIA: RICKSHAW RACE

MATERIALS

Wheelbarrow

INSTRUCTIONS

Have one child sit in the wheelbarrow and have another pull the wheelbarrow around the yard like a rickshaw. Or have the kids work in pairs to make "human wheelbarrows." One child holds their partner's legs so the first child can run using their arms.

FOOD IDEAS

- Lentils
- Naan bread
- Chai tea
- Samosas

CHINA: MAKE AND FLY A DRAGON KITE

MATERIALS

Paper kites

Markers

INSTRUCTIONS

Give each child a paper kite to decorate with Chinese dragons, or provide a pre-made kite that the kids can take turns flying in the yard.

FOOD IDEAS

- Noodles
- Wontons, pot stickers, or other dumplings
- Sweet and sour chicken

JAPAN: SUMO WRESTLING

MATERIALS

Pillows

INSTRUCTIONS

Create a circle, then have the children put pillows in their shirts and try to nudge one another out of the circle by bumping into one another with their bellies. Be sure to clear the space of anything dangerous and set some rules to prevent the children from getting hurt!

FOOD IDEAS

- Sushi
- Tofu
- Chicken katsu

"I see that it is by no means useless to travel, if a man wants to see something new."

—Jules Verne, *Around the World in Eighty Days*

USA: BASEBALL OR PANNING FOR GOLD

MATERIALS

Baseball or softball

Baseball bat

Gloves

Bases

Fake gold rocks (optional)

Plastic plates or aluminum pie tins (optional)

INSTRUCTIONS

Set up a mini baseball diamond. You can have all of the kids participate together since this is the last station. Just make sure everyone has a chance to hit the ball and run the bases. Or purchase some fake gold rocks at the local craft store, and bury them in dirt, so the children can find them by panning for gold with the plastic plates or pie tins.

FOOD IDEAS

• Hot dogs

• Hamburgers

• Popcorn

• Apple pie

PARTY FAVORS

The children will take home their passports filled with the memories of an epic day of travel. Here are a few ideas for additional parting gifts. Choose just one or put together a little gift bag with a souvenir from each country to remind them of their amazing race around the world.

• Tea (England)

• Papyrus or paper (Egypt)

• Elephant figurines (India)

• Chopsticks (China)

• Paper fans (Japan)

BY AINSLEY ARMENT

BLACK BEAUTY

BY ANNA SEWELL

As a student, I didn't love reading. I remember a teacher in high school telling me to read the CliffsNotes of a book because it would cover me for the test. It wasn't until I became the mother of a preschooler, seeking to find just the right schooling for my child, that I discovered the world of literature. Now I am overjoyed to read amazing books with my children. I get to fall into the pages with them, in laughter, tears, excitement, curiosity, and wonder.

Perhaps there is no greater experience than reading to—and with—our children because it produces rich conversation and meaningful connections while building character. Reading *Black Beauty* has indeed given us all of that and more.

THE GATHERING

A perfect setting for this book club is a beautiful historic ranch where you can tour horse stables. When we held our gathering, all of our senses were awakened as we smelled fresh hay, heard the horses chomping on carrots, and touched the iron horseshoes. If you can't get to horse stables, here are a few other ideas:

- A horse fair
- A horse supply store
- A friend's barn
- A garage that you can decorate and transform into a stable for the day (with some stuffed horses)

FOOD IDEAS

Keep the food simple and let the horse theme lead the way! Place quotes from the book beside each snack, and have the children take turns reading them before filling their plates.

- **APPLES**: "So, let us cheer up, and have a run to the other end of the orchard; I believe the wind has blown down some apples, and we might just as well eat them as the slugs."
- **OATMEAL COOKIES**: "He gave me some very nice oats, he patted me, spoke kindly, and then went away."
- **FRESHLY BAKED BAGUETTES AND A TRAY OF CARROTS**: "He would give me a piece of bread, which was very good,

and sometimes he brought a carrot for my mother."

- **WHEATGRASS**: "It was a great treat to us to be turned out into the home paddock or the old orchard; the grass was so cool and soft to our feet, the air so sweet, and the freedom to do as we liked was so pleasant—to gallop, to lie down, and roll over on our backs, or to nibble the sweet grass." (We served green grass juice to taste, along with some wheatgrass for those who were really brave!)

DISCUSSION QUESTIONS

Black Beauty offers the opportunity to discuss not only the characters, setting, and plot of the story but also heavy topics ranging from animal welfare to theology. We actually had to cut our discussion short, much to the disappointment of the children! How delightful is that? And what a testament to reading beautiful literature with our children. Oh, *Black Beauty*, we adore you.

1. Where does the story take place?

2. When does the story take place?

3. Why are the setting and date of the story important?

4. What are blinkers, and why were they used?

5. What does Black Beauty think of them?

6. What are bearing reins or checkreins, and why were they used?

7. What does Black Beauty think of them?

8. Who says this, and why: "I hope you will grow up gentle and good, and never learn bad ways; do your work with a good will, lift your feet up well when you trot, and never bite or kick even in play."

9. What are some of Black Beauty's names? Which name do you like the best? What would you have named him?

10. When Black Beauty is at Squire Gordon's home, the first horse he meets is described as "a little fat grey pony with a thick mane and tail, a very pretty head and a pert little nose." What is the name of this horse?

11. Whose lives does Black Beauty save, and how?

12. What did you learn from the book about horse care?

13. What are some things that Black Beauty eats?

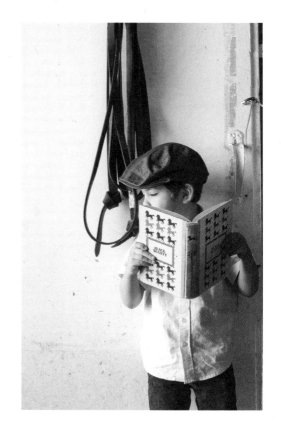

14. Who are the two ladies who become Black Beauty's last owners and what do they do when they realize they have Mrs. Gordon's favorite horse?

15. Who says this, and why: "You did right my boy, whether the fellow gets a summons or not. Many folks would have ridden by and said 'twas not their business to interfere. Now I say, that with cruelty and oppression it is everybody's business to interfere when they see it."

16. Have you ever intervened when you saw oppression? (Leave space for discussion about this).

17. Who says this, and why: "There is no religion without love, and people may talk as much as they like about their religion, but if it does not teach them to be good and kind to man and beast, it is all a sham." Do you agree? Why or why not?

HORSE RACE

MATERIALS

Brown paper bags

Newspaper

Branches (foraged nearby or brought along) or broom handles

String

Pennants

Ribbon for finish line

Die

Trophy

INSTRUCTIONS

Create stick horses for the kids to ride. Stuff brown paper bags with newspaper to make the heads, tie each head onto a branch or broom handle with string, and number the horses from 1 to 6 with pennants.

Up to six children can race at a time, with two children holding up a banner at the finish line and one child rolling a die. Whichever number the die lands on, that horse takes one giant leap forward. Whoever makes it to the finish line first wins a trophy. Repeat, passing off the trophy to each child who crosses the finish line.

PARTY FAVORS

- Corn seeds

  Give each kid a packet of corn seeds, or buy a few packages of seeds, provide small bags, and have each child pick out a handful of seeds.

- Horseshoes

  Give each kid a bag with a fresh paintbrush, paints, and a wooden horseshoe so they can create an artful masterpiece in honor of *Black Beauty*.

BY JENNIFER NARAKI

CHARLOTTE'S WEB

BY E. B. WHITE

A long with imagination, books develop our character. In *Charlotte's Web*, the powerful words that Charlotte uses to describe Wilbur are a valuable lesson in using our words to encourage those around us. And the way Charlotte is able to convince even an ill-tempered rat like Templeton to help save Wilbur inspires us to work on our own team spirit. Imagination, ideas, character, and nobility are the deeper benefits that come from sharing great books with our children.

THE GATHERING

A fun way to celebrate this book is by creating an old-time county fair. Find a nearby farm to visit so you can be near real animals, or set up a farm corner in your yard, complete with a miniature wheelbarrow, farm tools, and a stuffed pig.

Decorate by cutting 12 × 12-inch pieces of primary-color construction paper into 3 × 3-inch squares and then into pennant shapes, string with yarn, and tie onto outbuildings. Use gingham fabric for table coverings and blow up some balloons to add to the festive atmosphere.

FOOD IDEAS

Consider the following fair-themed treats:

- Big slices of cold watermelon
- Individual bags of popcorn
- A basket of apples
- Hot dogs or corn dogs
- "Templeton's egg cupcakes"—cupcakes decorated with green licorice and a candy egg
- Icy lemonade served in jelly jars

DISCUSSION QUESTIONS

1. What does Avery say Fern's pig is no bigger than?

2. How does Wilbur keep warm at night?

3. Where does Wilbur like to be when Fern is swimming?

4. What animals are in the barn with Wilbur?

5. Who helps Wilbur escape?

6. Why is Wilbur happy to meet Charlotte? How does Charlotte help Wilbur?

7. What does Wilbur want to avoid?

8. What words does Charlotte use to describe Wilbur?

9. How does the sheep convince Templeton to find words?

10. Why is Mrs. Arable worried about Fern?

11. According to Charlotte, what does "versatile" mean?

 **SAFETY TIP**

Using scissors can be dangerous and should be done with adult supervision.

12. What does Mrs. Zuckerman use to bathe Wilbur?

13. How does the sheep convince Templeton to go to the fair?

14. What kinds of warnings do the adults give Fern and Avery at the fair?

15. What is Charlotte's magnum opus?

16. Why does Charlotte say she is languishing?

17. Who wins the blue ribbon? What award does Wilbur win?

18. How do the Zuckermans and Arables feel about the award?

19. Why does Charlotte feel peaceful after Wilbur wins the award?

20. What does Wilbur name Charlotte's daughters?

EXHIBITS

MATERIALS

Removable putty

Outdoor tables

Blue ribbons

INSTRUCTIONS

County fairs have wonderful exhibits with artwork, flowers, and baked goods, and you can create your own. Ask each child to bring an exhibit. You can hang artwork with removable putty on the house walls and set up tables outside to display larger items. In our book club, my children created pictures related to the book, and we also displayed plants and flowers in our exhibit area. Have a guest judge award ribbons for each exhibit, being sure to have plenty of blue ribbons to go around.

CARNIVAL GAMES

Have plenty of prizes for every participant, and give free tickets to each child so they can play as often as they like. Here are some of the carnival games you can set up.

RING TOSS

MATERIALS

Old bottles

Wooden crate or bottle holder

Plastic bracelets

Prizes

INSTRUCTIONS

Gather old bottles and stand them in a wooden crate or bottle holder. Use simple plastic bracelets for the rings. Award a prize for each participant.

FISH BOWL

MATERIALS

Feeder goldfish

Jelly jars

Ping-Pong balls

INSTRUCTIONS

Purchase feeder goldfish and place them in short jelly jars filled with water. Use Ping-Pong balls for tossing and give each child plenty of chances to win a fish.

CUPCAKE WALK

MATERIALS

Sidewalk chalk

Paper

Pen

Music

Cupcakes (one for each child)

INSTRUCTIONS

Use sidewalk chalk to write numbers on a driveway or patio. Write the same numbers on slips of paper. Have the children walk around the driveway or patio while the music plays and freeze in place when the music stops. Select a number at random. The child standing on the selected number wins a cupcake and is eliminated from the game, giving all of the players a chance to win.

SPIDERWEB WORDS

MATERIALS

Yarn

White glue

Waxed paper

Watercolor (optional)

Cardstock (optional)

Clothespins (optional)

INSTRUCTIONS

Use yarn to make a large web between two trees or posts. Have the children use lots of white glue and yarn on waxed paper to write some of the words that Charlotte uses to describe Wilbur. When dry, tie the words onto the web. Or give the children examples of watercolor lettering and let them use the technique to write the words onto cardstock. Pin the cardstock to the web with the clothespins.

"Children pay better attention than grownups. If Fern says that the animals in Zuckerman's barn talk, I'm quite ready to believe her."

—E. B. White, *Charlotte's Web*

CLAY ANIMALS

MATERIALS

Sculpey or air-dry clay
Toothpicks

INSTRUCTIONS

The simple body shapes of Templeton and Wilbur are easy to create with clay. Make an oval-shaped body with clay, then use toothpicks to attach a head, a tail, and feet. For Charlotte, make a round ball with a smaller ball for the head, and add eight legs.

PARTY FAVORS

- Small tin buckets to hold the prizes from games
- Caramel apples or personal-size watermelons
- Paper cones of nuts or cotton candy
- Small packets of toy farm animals
- A few bars of clay to make their own toy animals
- Toy spiders and small balls of yarn for making webs

BY JENNIFER PEPITO

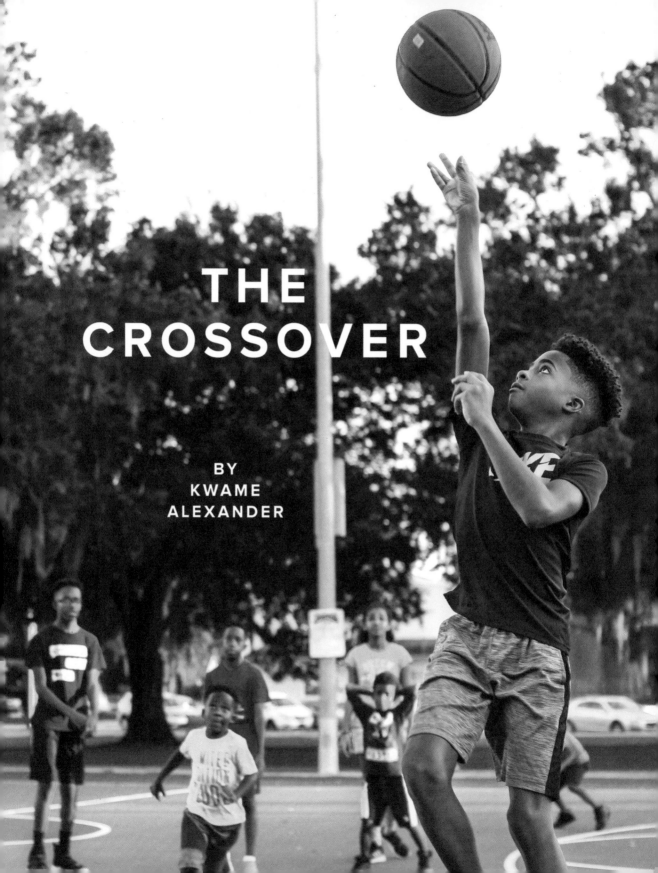

THE
CROSSOVER

BY
KWAME
ALEXANDER

When Kwame Alexander first released the novel *The Crossover*, I was drawn to it because it was written completely in verse. Being a lover of words and of poetry, I was intrigued by a book that would tell a complete story in this extraordinary way. Then, when I sat down to read it with my children, we just could not put it down. We read the whole thing in one sitting!

The subject of much of the book is basketball, which seamlessly weaves the poems together. My children and I felt like the spectators at a game, watching the rise and fall of action of the players on a court. At the end of each chapter, my children would gently urge me to read on until we reached the very last word, by which point no one wanted to move. We were united through the poetic plot, connected through its characters, and bonded through our conversations as the tale unfolded. We all emerged with a new understanding of brotherhood, friendship, family, and life.

One of the heavier topics in the novel is heart health. You can use this as an opportunity to discuss with children things like what to do if you suspect someone might be having a heart attack.

THE GATHERING

Since basketball is such a strong component of this story, the ideal location for this gathering is at a park with a basketball court and some tables, though you could easily have it in a backyard as well. If a basketball hoop isn't available, a makeshift one can be constructed out of a bucket or basket for the games.

Play jazz and/or hip-hop as the background music for your literature celebration. Some artists mentioned in the book are Dizzy Gillespie, Horace Silver, John Coltrane, Tupac, Jay-Z, Kanye, and Lil Wayne.

For decor, reprint the ten poems called "Basketball Rules," and hang them up around the gathering space or place them on the tables.

FOOD IDEAS

These are some of the foods mentioned throughout the story. A combination of any of them would make a great party menu:

- Chinese food
- Chicken and barbecue
- Mac and cheese
- Collard greens
- Roasted turkey
- Tuna salad on wheat
- Pita bread and hummus
- Vegetable lasagna
- Sweet potato pie
- Krispy Kreme doughnuts
- Iced tea

DISCUSSION QUESTIONS

1. Why do you think Kwame Alexander decided to write the entire book in verse? How does it add to or take away from the story?

2. This book is also available as a graphic novel. If you have a chance to compare the two versions, discuss which experience you enjoyed more as a reader. What does the graphic novel format add to or take away from the story?

3. Music is important in the story. Dad loves jazz, and the twins love hip-hop. How are the rhythms of jazz and hip-hop connected to the poems throughout the novel? Can poetry have a rhythm? How?

4. How would you describe Josh and Jordan's relationship? How does it change throughout the story?

5. The Bell family really connects over sports, specifically basketball. Is there something over which your family connects?

6. How do the family members bring balance to one another? How do you see balance working in your family relationships?

7. How important is Josh's hair to him? Reread "Ode to My Hair" if necessary. How is his hair connected to his basketball playing? How do you think Josh feels when he has to cut off his locks because of his brother's carelessness? How does this compare with the event that happens later when Josh gives Jordan a bloody nose during a game?

8. Why do you think Mr. Bell is so against going to see a doctor? How do his family members each feel about his position? What would be your reaction if you were a part of their family?

9. How does Dr. Crystal Bell (Jordan and Josh's mom) attempt to manage the family's health? Do you think her efforts are appreciated? How does her family react?

10. JB and Filthy McNasty are the boys' nicknames. How did they get them? Do you have a nickname?

11. Why do you think Josh begins to dislike being called Filthy McNasty?

12. When Jordan begins to spend a lot of time with Alexis (Miss Sweet Tea), Josh admits to feeling lonely. How does Josh handle Jordan's feelings about Alexis? How does Jordan handle Josh's feelings about his relationship?

13. How would you describe Coach Hawkins's role in the story? What kind of relationship does he have with the students/players?

14. Dad's Basketball Rule #10 is:

A loss is inevitable,

like snow in winter.

True champions

learn

to dance

through

the storm

How does this poem fit into Josh and Jordan's life? How is the rule related to the loss they experience at the end of the story?

15. Why do you think it takes so long for Jordan to forgive Josh? What is it that finally makes his heart begin to change?

16. This novel is full of vocabulary poems (poems that introduce new words). Do the vocabulary poems help you understand the meaning of the words? How do they help push the story along?

17. Why do you think the book is titled *The Crossover*?

CROSSOVER DRIBBLE

MATERIALS

Music

Basketball

INSTRUCTIONS

All the players stand in a circle. When the music starts, the player with the ball has to dribble crossover style—switching the ball from one hand to the other—and then pass the ball to the next person (decide before the game if you will be passing to the right or to the left). When the music stops, the person holding the ball is out. Continue until there is one winner.

LAYUP DRILL

MATERIALS

Basketball

Basketball hoop

INSTRUCTIONS

Divide everyone into two lines facing the basket. One line of players will be doing the layup shots (off the backboard into the hoop), and the other will be rebounding the ball (retrieving it after the shot). Decide which side will do each activity.

The first person in both lines comes up to the basket. The person from the layup line dribbles the ball and makes the layup shot. The partner from the other line rebounds the ball and then passes it to the next person in the layup line. Each player returns to the back of the *opposite* line. The first players in each line continue in the same fashion until the drill is over.

FREE THROWS IN A ROW

MATERIALS

Tape (optional)

Multiple basketballs

Basketball hoop

Timer

INSTRUCTIONS

Decide where the free throw line will be if you are not on an actual court. Mark off the line with tape. Each player gets 20 seconds to stand at the free throw line and try to toss the ball into the basket. The player continues to toss balls until the time is up. The winner is the player to make the most shots. Be sure to have some other children willing to rebound the balls and toss them back to the person shooting, especially if you don't have many basketballs.

PIPE CLEANER CHAMPIONSHIP RINGS

MATERIALS

Pipe cleaners

White glue

Plastic gems or sequins

INSTRUCTIONS

Have each child place their desired finger on top of a pipe cleaner, right at the center. Help the child create a fitted loop by twisting the ends around each other right where the pipe cleaner meets the finger. Make sure the loop is not too tight and the ring can be removed easily. After the loop is created, twist and tuck the leftover ends into a flat, circular shape that sits on top of the finger. Use tacky glue to attach some gems or sequins to give the championship ring a little pizzazz.

CHA-CHA SLIDE

MATERIALS

Music

Online video showing "Cha-Cha Slide" dance

INSTRUCTIONS

In *The Crossover*, Coach is blasting "his favorite dance music, and before you know it, we're all doing the Cha-Cha Slide." Show everyone the video on your phone or a computer, and have a little fun together dancing the Cha-Cha Slide.

CONCRETE POETRY

MATERIALS

Paper

Pens or pencils

Scissors

INSTRUCTIONS

In concrete poetry, the way that the poem is arranged visually on the page adds significance to what the poem is conveying with words. For example, a writer might convey the word "down" by making the word travel down the page in a way that causes your eyes to do the same. Or a writer might write a poem about a tree in the shape of a tree, with the words arranged around the outline of the shape.

Kwame Alexander artfully infuses the novel with many examples of concrete poetry. With copies of the book available to reference, have children try writing a concrete poem of their own. For younger children, you may need to create a shape for them

on which they can write (or you can transcribe) their words.

Another option is to have the children create a poem with a partner. Make a list of favorite words or lines from the story. Write them on paper and then cut them out into strips. Next, work together to rearrange the strips into a poem on which both partners agree. Make final edits, adding necessary words or phrases.

 SAFETY TIP

Using scissors can be dangerous and should be done with adult supervision.

PARTY FAVORS

Kids can take home the championship rings they created. Another fun idea is poetry tiles. Give each child a small burlap bag filled with ten words to inspire poetry. Print the words on cardstock and cut them into rectangles. You can put magnetic tape on the back of each word, so the children can explore creating poems on a magnetic surface, like a refrigerator.

BY LESLIE MARTINO

ESPERANZA RISING

BY PAM MUÑOZ RYAN

Esperanza Rising is a beautiful story of survival, perseverance, and rising above one's challenges. I hold this story close to my heart as my own parents emigrated from Mexico in the 1950s and for a short time worked as farm laborers when they first arrived in the US. As in this story, my parents faced many challenges as they came to a new country where they didn't speak the language and the culture was so different from their own. They worked hard and sacrificed much, instilling their hopes and dreams in their children. The accomplishments of my siblings and me, and then of our children, are due in large part to my parents and all that they overcame.

Esperanza Rising presents an opportunity to learn about a different culture and the life of immigrants and farm laborers. It opens the door to great conversations about new beginnings, discrimination, classism, perseverance, family bonds, sacrifice, and overcoming hardships and challenges.

If you enjoy audiobooks, I would highly recommend listening to this one. There are many Spanish phrases and words in this book, and the narrator, Trini Alvarado, does a beautiful job of reading the story and bringing the characters to life.

THE GATHERING

The gathering can be held in a home, backyard, or local park. What matters most is celebrating family and friendship with good food, which is very important in *Esperanza Rising*. You can play Mexican music in the background and include "Las Mañanitas," the birthday song. Decorations can be simple, including roses in vases or jars, small piñatas, and fruit centerpieces.

FOOD IDEAS

Put together a fun Mexican feast based on the Mexican dishes mentioned in the book and the fruits and vegetables named in the chapter titles. Your feast can include the following:

- Enchiladas
- Beans and rice
- Guacamole
- Chips and salsa
- Fruits such as grapes, figs, guavas, cantaloupes, plums, and peaches

- Cucumbers with lime, chili powder, and salt
- Flour tortillas
- Flan
- Jamaica (hibiscus tea)

DISCUSSION QUESTIONS

1. When and where does the story take place?

2. What is life like for Esperanza and her family in Mexico?

3. Why does Mamá feel they must leave Mexico?

4. Esperanza tells Miguel that a deep river runs between them. What does she mean by this? What do they have in common? What are their differences? Do her feelings change later in the story?

5. Why can't Abuelita leave Mexico with Esperanza and Mamá?

6. How do Esperanza and her family have to travel when they leave Mexico?

7. Carmen, the woman on the train, says that she is rich even though she is poor. What does she mean by this?

8. Once they arrive in California, who picks up Esperanza's family, and what part do they play in the family's lives?

9. How do living conditions change for Esperanza and Mamá once they are in the United States?

10. How would you feel if you had to move to another country that was very different from your own?

11. What surprise do Alfonso and Miguel bring along with them from Aguascalientes for Esperanza and Mamá?

12. What happens to Mamá after the dust storm?

13. Why do Miguel and Esperanza drive to the Japanese market that is farther away?

14. Why does Marta want to strike? What does she want to change?

15. Isabel has the best grades in her class. Why doesn't she win Queen of May Day? What does Esperanza do to try and help her feel better?

16. Esperanza works on the zigzag crochet blanket that Abuelita started in Mexico. How does the zigzag pattern reflect the mountains and valleys of her life?

17. Why does Miguel take Esperanza's money orders, which she had been saving?

18. At the end of the story, Esperanza can feel the earth's heart beating just as she had at the beginning of the story with Papá. What do you think this means?

19. Isabel shows her uneven crochet stitches to Esperanza. Esperanza gently pulls her stitches apart and tells her, "Do not ever be afraid to start over." How does this tie into the theme of the book?

ACTIVITIES

YARN DOLLS

MATERIALS

Yarn

Scissors

INSTRUCTIONS

There are instructions to make your own yarn doll in the back of *Esperanza Rising*. We modified them a bit to reflect how Mamá and Esperanza made yarn dolls in the story together.

1. Cut seven 12-inch-long pieces of yarn and set them aside.

2. Have a friend hold their hands out, a couple of inches apart, palms facing up. Wrap your yarn around your friend's hands 50 times.

3. Cut the yarn to separate it from the ball.

4. Slip one of your 12-inch pieces of yarn through the middle of the loops (between the top and bottom strands) and tie a tight knot.

5. Pull the yarn off of your friend's hands.

6. Hold your yarn loop with the tie at the top. This is the top of your doll's head.

7. Using another of your 12-inch pieces, make the head by tying it around all 100 strands about an inch or two below your first knot.

8. Cut the bottom loops.

9. Create an arm by braiding together twelve strands right below the head. Use another of your 12-inch pieces to secure the braid at the bottom.

10. Repeat on the other side to create another arm.

11. With another of your 12-inch pieces, tie a knot a couple of inches below the head to form the torso. If you leave your doll this way, it will look as if it's wearing a dress or skirt, or you can separate the remaining strands in half and braid them to create legs. Trim all ends to make them even.

 **SAFETY TIP**

Using scissors can be dangerous and should be done with adult supervision.

CROCHETING

MATERIALS

Yarn

Crochet hooks

Scissors

INSTRUCTIONS

Some members of your book club may already know how to crochet. Encourage them to teach the others how to crochet a simple chain or a new stitch. You can even try the zigzag pattern that Abuelita uses in the book.

 SAFETY TIP

Using scissors can be dangerous and should be done with adult supervision.

MAKE FLOUR TORTILLAS

INSTRUCTIONS

Freshly made flour tortillas are the best! Most recipes require just a few simple ingredients: flour, salt, baking powder, oil, and water. Find a recipe online that speaks to you, and share the experience of making flour tortillas with your book club.

LEARN THE SPANISH NAMES OF FRUITS

MATERIALS

Pens

Paper

INSTRUCTIONS

Write out the names of the fruits mentioned in the book in both Spanish and English, and learn them together.

PARTY FAVORS

The children can take home the yarn dolls that they make at the gathering. Here are two additional ideas for party favors:

• Bookmarks with a Mexican proverb
• Hibiscus tea bags

BY NAOMI OVANDO

THE EVOLUTION OF CALPURNIA TATE

BY
JACQUELINE KELLY

Our book club had decided to read *The Evolution of Calpurnia Tate* and meet up for a hike through a cypress hammock. By the time we reached our lovely book club spot next to the cypress dome, all desire to have a controlled discussion fled. I watched children eagerly spread blankets and pull out microscopes to study the pond water. Little ones were chasing the ever-present cloud of crickets, and older boys were moving rocks and branches and settling down to sketch in their nature journals.

I smiled when I realized that we had been discussing our book the entire time. Book clubs aren't just about snacks and discussion questions. The heart of a book club is how the book motivates, expands, shapes, and inspires us into action, which I saw firsthand that day.

THE GATHERING

Calpurnia's adventures and scientific inquiries often take place out in nature, so this is a great book club gathering for outdoors. You could meet in a nearby forest, field, or park or near a stream or lake. Let nature do the decorating for you! And since Calpurnia's relationship with her grandfather is central to the story, invite grandparents or older friends to join you and share the great outdoors together.

FOOD IDEAS

- Pecan pie
- Lemon meringue pie
- Lemonade
- Ants on a log
- Blue Jell-O cups with gummy worms
- Other insect-theme snacks

DISCUSSION QUESTIONS

1. What are some lessons about scientific observation that we learn from Granddaddy and Calpurnia's adventures?

2. In addition to their shared interest in science and nature, what do Callie and her grandfather have in common?

3. Callie's grandfather seems to take more of an interest in her than her brothers. Why do you think this is?

4. Granddaddy fought in the war. How do you think his experiences affect his relationship with Viola?

5. What was your favorite nature interaction in the story?

6. Calpurnia always claims Granddaddy and Harry as "mine," and she gets nervous when other people come between them. Why does she act this way?

7. After an unsuccessful experiment, Granddaddy says, "The day the experiment succeeds is the day the experiment ends. And I inevitably find that the sadness of the ending outweighs the celebration of success." How does this quote relate to Granddaddy's re-action upon receiving the letter from the Smithsonian?

8. What changes does Calpurnia go through in the book?

9. How does this story inspire you?

10. Discuss the meaning of the quotes at the beginning of each chapter. How are they important to the book as a whole?

11. Callie writes a list of things she would like to see before she dies. What kinds of things would you like to see?

12. Describe your best day in nature.

13. How does Callie change throughout the story as a result of her science studies?

ACTIVITIES

MICROSCOPIC EXPLORATION

MATERIALS

Pipettes

Water from a creek, lake, or other body of water

Slides

Microscope

Journals or paper and drawing materials (optional)

INSTRUCTIONS

Using a pipette, place a drop of water on a slide, put it under the microscope, and let the kids observe. You can also have them record what they find in their journals or draw it on a piece of paper.

WILDLIFE JOURNALING

MATERIALS

Notebook or journal

Pens and pencils

INSTRUCTIONS

Find a grassy field. Invite the children to sit still for 5 to 10 minutes and record all the wildlife they see.

BUG COLLECTING

MATERIALS

Insect houses

Jars

Notebook or journal

Pens and pencils

INSTRUCTIONS

Collect various insects and tiny creatures to view and sketch together.

PARTY FAVORS

- Caterpillars in jars for observation
- Small notebooks and pens to use as a field journal
- Bags of gummy worms

BY ELSIE IUDICELLO

MOTHER-DAUGHTER BOOK CLUB

BY RENEE HUSTON

When my daughter became old enough to read and discuss chapter books, I mentioned to her the possibility of starting a mother-daughter book club, which piqued her curiosity. We made a list of friends around her age and sent an invitational email asking if anyone might want to join our monthly book club.

Our idea was simple: we'd meet once per month as mothers and daughters, and each meeting would be led by a different mother-daughter duo. They would be in charge of choosing the book, hosting the meeting (or finding a suitable location), and creating an atmosphere to discuss the book together. We had an overwhelming response, and thus the Rainbow Readers Book Club (name selected by the girls) began.

My daughter and I are in our third year of leading our fellow bookworms, and we are having a wonderful time making memories together through books. The girls are various ages, and since the moms have also read the book, they participate in the discussions too.

Here are a few tips for starting your own mother-daughter book club.

SET A PREDICTABLE TIME, DATE, AND BOOK SCHEDULE

We meet the same Friday of each month, September through May (skipping December). An evening time frame works best for us so dads can help out with our other children. I collect all the book choices in August and create a schedule for the school year, taking into consideration the genre and length of each book. (I recommend not scheduling two long books back-to-back.)

CHOOSE A VARIETY OF BOOKS

Consider reading books of various lengths, authors, and genres. It's encouraging to hear when one of the girls has explored more books by an author that she had never heard of before or is suddenly into mystery books after being introduced to them at book club.

BE OKAY WITH EACH MEETING BEING DIFFERENT

One of the things that I love about having a different mom and daughter lead each month is that no two meetings look the same! Some lead wonderfully rich book discussions while others love to incorporate crafts, games, or baked goods that correspond with the book choice. Everyone's individual talents shine, and we moms get an opportunity to teach our daughters about leadership and hospitality.

TAKE THE MEETING ON THE ROAD

Sometimes a field trip matches up nicely with our book choice. For instance, we vis-ited a local horse rescue after reading *Riding Freedom*, and *Charlotte's Web* spurred us on to meet at a petting farm and take a hayride.

HAVE FUN AND MAKE MEMORIES WITH YOUR DAUGHTER!

Make it clear at the beginning that you expect the moms to read the books each month too. Some of our moms use the book as their family's monthly read-aloud, while others with older girls each grab their own copies and read it independently. It's fun to listen to recorded books too. These are precious memories to make together.

FARMER BOY

BY LAURA INGALLS
WILDER

have loved the book *Farmer Boy* since I was a little girl. I remember sitting on the couch with my mom as she read it aloud to me. It was an instant favorite. Throughout my girlhood, I read it several times on my own, snuggled in bed or sitting up in my tree house.

When I had two young sons, I read it to them, and they wanted to know why they couldn't have pie for breakfast every day like Almanzo. But it was reading *Farmer Boy* with all five of my children that meant the most to me.

We laughed together when the Wilder kids ate almost all of the sugar. We were on the edge of our seats when the schoolteacher took on the town bullies. And we all rejoiced with Almanzo when he finally got his colts. To be reading a book I loved as a child, a book so packed with sweet memories, with all of my children gathered around me felt like I was living out one of my most cherished parenting dreams.

THE GATHERING

You can host a *Farmer Boy* book club just about anywhere: inside a home, at a park, or on a farm. Giving children a chance to interact with animals is an added bonus.

FOOD IDEAS

You cannot read *Farmer Boy* without your taste buds watering, as the author describes the meals the Wilders shared, from ham and gravy, boiled potatoes, and salt pork to sausage cakes, flapjacks, homemade doughnuts, big yellow cheeses, and every pie imaginable. You can actually google "Every meal Almanzo eats in Laura Ingalls Wilder's *Farmer Boy*" for ideas to suit your gathering, whether it's

a small party with lunch or a larger party with snacks.

- Chicken and dumplings
- Warm homemade bread
- Ham
- Apples
- Cheese
- Popcorn
- Apple cider
- Milk
- Pumpkin pie

DISCUSSION QUESTIONS

1. What are some of the food items mentioned in the book that you want to eat or learn how to make?

2. How does Almanzo's place in the family shape the chores he wants to do?

3. Why are the horses so important to Almanzo? Why does his father make him work with the oxen first? Have you ever had to show that you were proficient in one area in order to do the work you wanted to do?

4. What do you think about Almanzo's daily schedule? How is it similar to yours, and how is it different? What parts of his day do you wish you could incorporate into yours?

5. The seasons are very important to the order of the Wilders' days. Do the seasons change the rhythm of your days? What season is your favorite, and why?

6. Much of the story takes place in the barn. How does it stay so warm in the winter? What are some of the Wilder family's special barn rules?

7. When Almanzo's parents leave, what rule is the hardest for the children to keep? How do they cover up their transgression? Do you feel you and your siblings would handle this situation in a similar way?

8. Why is Almanzo so upset in the days after his parents return? What does this show about his character? What do you learn about his siblings' characters?

9. The Hardscrabble Boys act very differently than the Wilder children. How do you feel about their behavior in class and the steps taken to stop it?

10. How does the location of the Wilder family's home help or hinder them in obtaining items for the farm and in selling their products? How does their situation compare to what you've read about pioneers who lived farther west during the same period?

11. There is much excitement when the tin man comes to the Wilder farmstead. Is there an event or visitor that your family looks forward to every year?

12. Have you ever been to a county fair? What did you most enjoy? How was your experience compared with Almanzo's?

13. Do you feel that the way Almanzo grows his prized pumpkin is fair? What do you think about how he handles himself when asked about it?

14. Almanzo and Royal, as the only boys in the family, have a special relationship. How are they similar, and how are they different?

HAND-DIPPED BEESWAX CANDLES

Almanzo's mother filled large kettles with beef fat, which melted into tallow. The Wilders used the tallow to make all of the candles they would need for the coming year. We loved the idea of making our own candles, so we decided to give it a try. We used beeswax instead of tallow and found they burn brighter, remove toxins from the air, and have the most delightful scent of sweet honeycomb.

MATERIALS

A 1-pound block of beeswax

Spool of candlewicking thread

A tall can or metal carafe that can be devoted to melted beeswax

INSTRUCTIONS

1. Fill a large saucepan with water and simmer over low heat.

2. Put the beeswax in the tin can and place the can in the water.

3. After the wax melts, remove the pot from the burner and place it on a heat-resistant surface.

4. Dip a piece of candlewicking thread into the hot wax, and let it air-dry.

5. Repeat this process three or four times, allowing the thread to air-dry between each quick dip.

6. Using your fingers, gently straighten the thread as it sets. Let it cool completely.

7. Continue to dip your candle in the hot wax, letting it cool between dips so that it solidifies. Be sure to remove your candle quickly so the hot wax does not melt your hard work away.

8. Keep dipping until the candle has reached the desired size and shape.

TIPS

- Leave extra wick at the top to create a loop so the candle can be hung to dry.
- Get several candles going for younger children who don't have the patience to wait for results.

- Use a container to store the extra melted beeswax for next time.
- Fill a pitcher with ice water and alternate dipping the candle in hot wax and cold water.

- The trick to more uniform candles is letting the wax cool completely between dips.

POPCORN AND MILK EXPERIMENT

"You can fill a glass full to the brim with milk and fill another glass of the same size brim full of popcorn, and then you can put all the popcorn kernel by kernel into the milk, and the milk will not run over. You cannot do this with bread. Popcorn and milk are the only two things that will go into the same place."
—Laura Ingalls Wilder, *Farmer Boy*

My kids found this passage fascinating and were eager to try it for themselves. As it turns out, it's true! We enjoyed a lively discussion about why this might be so. These little talks always end up being my favorite part of any book club gathering with children. Try this experiment at your own!

SOFT VANILLA ICE CREAM

Although we made our ice cream in zip-lock bags and not with an old-fashioned hand crank mixer like Almanzo and his siblings, the kids were still delighted to make ice cream from scratch.

INGREDIENTS

½ cup half-and-half

1 tablespoon sugar

¼ teaspoon vanilla

3 cups crushed ice

⅓ cup rock salt

INSTRUCTIONS

1. Put the half-and-half, sugar, and vanilla into a sandwich-size ziplock bag, and seal it tightly. (We sealed ours with duct tape.)

2. Put the ice and rock salt in a gallon-size ziplock bag, and then add the small filled bag. Seal the large bag tightly. (We used duct tape for this too.)

3. Squeeze the bag until the ice cream thickens, about 10 to 15 minutes. Have the children work in teams of two so they can take turns squeezing the bag when their hands get cold.

4. Remove the small bag, unseal it carefully so that no salty water gets inside, and pour the soft-serve ice cream into cups to eat with a spoon or drink.

PARTY FAVORS

Print out the ice cream recipe so that the kids can make it again at home.

BY GRETA ESKRIDGE

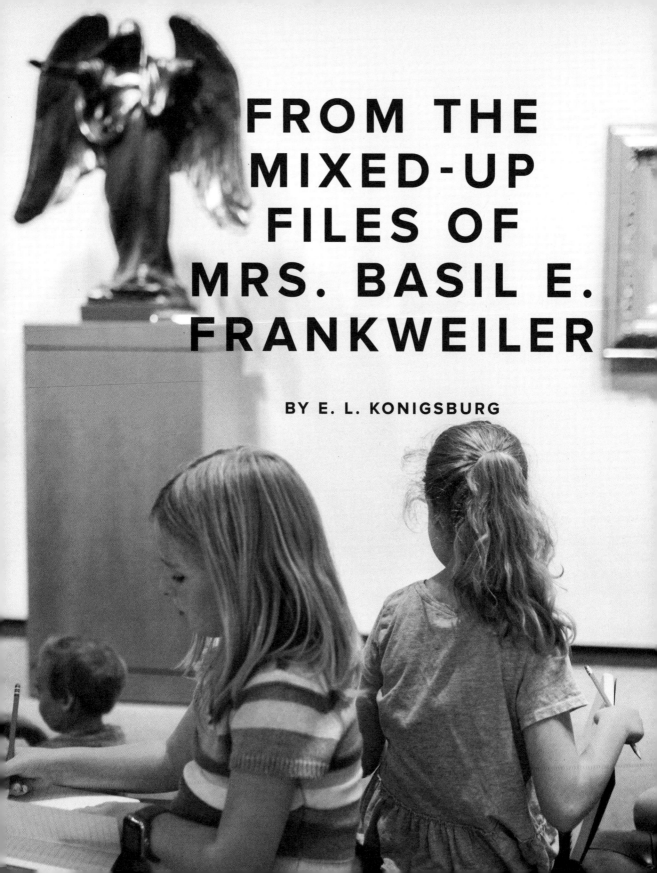

FROM THE MIXED-UP FILES OF MRS. BASIL E. FRANKWEILER

BY E. L. KONIGSBURG

At the heart of *From the Mixed-Up Files of Mrs. Basil E. Frankweiler*, we see the deepening bond of two very different siblings, Claudia and her brother Jamie, as they run away to live in the Metropolitan Museum of Art and work through challenges together. "What happened was: they became a team, a family of two," the author writes. *The Mixed-Up Files* helps us treasure the unexpected experiences that foster teamwork in our families, whether it is the car trip that takes twice as long as it should have or the tent that leaks in the middle of the night. These shared adventures position us side by side, forcing us to work together toward the same goal.

THE GATHERING

If you have access to a museum, that is the ideal location. You can do the bulk of the activities and discussion outside the museum, at a nearby park, or even at home before or after the trip, to allow for noise and mess. Check with your museum to see if there are any special tours or resources for school-age visitors. If you don't have a museum or gallery nearby, consider meeting at a home that is rich in artwork. Or allow the children to create pieces of their own to hang on a wall that can serve as a museum backdrop.

FOOD IDEAS

- **HOT FUDGE SUNDAES:** To save money for her train fare, Claudia skips more than three weeks of hot fudge sundaes, but you don't have to! You can create a simple sundae with one flavor of ice cream and chocolate syrup, or your group can have an ice cream bar where everyone brings a favorite topping to share.

- **"VENDING MACHINE" SNACKS:** Claudia and Jamie use the vending machine for many meals. Construct a "vending machine" out of a box or small shelf, and stock it with a variety of snacks with assigned prices. Give each participant "money" to purchase selections with, which will allow them to exercise choice and practice their math skills. Snack ideas include crackers, chips, pretzels, granola bars, dried fruit, and trail mix.

- **MACARONI AND CHEESE:** While the children are at Mrs. Frankweiler's home, the butler announces the meal as "nouilles et fromage en casserole," which turns out to be macaroni and cheese. Serve macaroni and cheese at your gathering, and ask the children to think of and share fancy names for otherwise ordinary foods.

DISCUSSION QUESTIONS

1. Who is telling the story? Why do you think it is written this way?

2. Why do you think Claudia wants to run away from home?

3. Do you think the museum is a good choice for a destination? If not, what would be a better place?

4. If you were going on an adventure and could pick only one person to be your partner, who would you want to bring with you?

5. How do you think Mr. and Mrs. Kincaid feel when Claudia and Jamie run away?

6. If you had to live in a museum, what would you do the same as the children? What would you do differently?

7. If you ran away to a museum, what section would you want to study?

8. Why do you think Claudia was captivated by the angel statue? What is something you have seen that you have really loved?

9. What does the word "homesick" mean to you? Have you ever been homesick?

10. In what ways are you like Claudia or Jamie?

11. What did you think about Mrs. Frankweiler? Is her character what you expected it to be?

12. What is your opinion of Claudia and Jamie's relationship? What makes for a good sibling relationship?

13. How do Claudia and Jamie change during the story?

14. What is your favorite part of the book?

ACTIVITIES

These activities tap into scenes from the book. For example, Jamie and Claudia use a typewriter to communicate with the museum staff, and Jamie plays the card game War with his friend Bruce on the bus.

EXPLORE A TYPEWRITER

MATERIALS

Typewriter
Paper or small cards

INSTRUCTIONS

Supply a typewriter and paper or cards and allow everyone a chance to type a quote from the book or a message of their own.

WAR CARD GAME

MATERIALS

Decks of cards (one for each pair of kids)
Prize (optional)

INSTRUCTIONS

Review the rules online before the gathering so you can explain it to the kids. Pair up the kids for a War tournament. Offer a small prize to the winner.

CLAY ANGELS

MATERIALS

Modeling clay

INSTRUCTIONS

Sculpt angels from modeling clay. A wonderful video on YouTube called "10 Minute Angel Sculpture Demonstration by Mathilda Tanner" offers a simple tutorial for all ages.

SKETCHING

MATERIALS

Pictures of artwork

Notebook or paper

Pens and pencils

INSTRUCTIONS

Prompt each participant to closely observe and sketch a work of art. Consider using a piece by Michelangelo or a statue or painting of an angel.

INSTRUMENT CASE GAME

MATERIALS

Instrument cases

Clothes and other small items to pack

INSTRUCTIONS

Provide each person or team with an instrument case and set out a variety of garments and items that could be used for a trip. See who can pack the most into their case in the allotted time, say 30 or 60 seconds.

ADJECTIVES ACTIVITY

MATERIALS

Index cards (one per child)

Pen or pencil

White glue

Craft sticks (one per child)

INSTRUCTIONS

Before the gathering, prepare an index card for each child. On one side of the card, write "Claudia," and on the other side write "Jamie." Glue each card to a craft stick. For the activity, give each participant a card. Review what adjectives are, and then read a word from the following list. Ask the children to use their card to show if they think the adjective best describes Claudia or Jamie. Repeat. This activity is a great way to open up discussion about the characters, as there are no right or wrong answers.

- Brave
- Wise
- Adventurous
- Curious
- Careful
- Polite
- Ambitious
- Independent
- Disciplined
- Detail-oriented
- Serious
- Funny

PARTY FAVORS

- Postcards or small prints of a famous work of art
- Small coin purses with some loose change for snacks (easier than fishing it out of the fountain!)

BY MANDY LACKEY

THE GREEN EMBER

BY S. D. SMITH

My children and I have returned to this tale again and again, gleaning more with each visit. Reading *The Green Ember* is like pouring courage down your children's spine and igniting a fire for truth, goodness, and beauty in their heart. As we read, my boys began to crave the life and character of a hero. This is incredible because the floppy-eared rabbit heroes spend the majority of the book fleeing from evil and hiding in caves, a hair's breadth from death at every turn. But their goodness shines brilliantly, even as they navigate difficult human issues, such as deep-seated anger and shattering loss. And it is this light in the midst of terrible darkness that draws children in.

My eldest remarked, "This book gives me a craving to be a hero. Something about it makes me imagine that I can fight for good things and protect good things and make good things, even though I am just a kid right now. When bad stuff happens, I can still do good things."

In other words, this is a book that treats children with respect. S. D. Smith delivers the story with a truth and honesty that is

reassuring. Yes, evil is real. Yes, it is out there. And yes, it can be beaten.

THE GATHERING

This book club gathering can be done inside the house. Ask kids to come in costume. My boys were cloaked in old brown bed sheets. A little girl wore a velvet dress. One boy came in full Robin Hood garb with the whimsical touch of bunny ears. Swords made of sticks and twine were tucked into belts. A few kids brandished swords made from pool noodles.

FOOD IDEAS

- Veggie soup
- Banana bread
- Carrots and hummus
- Carrot cake
- Lemonade or cider
- Cookies

DISCUSSION QUESTIONS

1. Describe Heather and Picket's home and life in Nick Hollow.

2. Discuss their relationship as events unfold in the hollow and they begin their escape.

3. This story deals with many first impressions. What were your first impressions of Smalls, Helmer, and Kyle? How did your feelings toward these characters change as you read the book?

4. How does Picket change over the course of the story? Can you relate to his anger? What ultimately helps Picket work through his feelings?

5. Why do the residents of the mountain look to the Mended Wood at all times? What is the significance of the guilds?

6. Do you have a favorite minor character? Tell us about them. Why are they your favorite?

7. What truth do Picket and Heather discover about their family? How does it change them?

8. Talk about redemption. What does the word mean? Where do we see redemption in this story?

9. Discuss the events surrounding the final battle.

10. What do you think "bear the flame" means?

ACTIVITIES

STAR SEEK

MATERIALS

Sticks

Twine

Red yarn or ribbons

INSTRUCTIONS

Fashion a star out of sticks and twine, and tie red yarn or ribbons to its center. Find a field or meadow, and let your star fly like Heather and Picket!

SWORD FIGHT WITH HOMEMADE SWORDS

MATERIALS

Sticks or pool noodles

Twine

Foam swords (optional)

INSTRUCTIONS

Some kids might bring toy swords from home. For those who don't or for a fun craft, have them make their own by tying together sticks or pool noodles with twine (or provide some foam swords from a dollar store). When all the children are armed, let them have a ball out in a big open field.

HELMER'S TREE

MATERIALS

Cardboard

Pens or markers

Rope

Blunt swords for play (see "Sword Fight" for instructions)

INSTRUCTIONS

Draw enemy birds or wolves on cardboard and tie them to tree branches with rope. Invite the children to use their homemade swords to train under the tree. Eager boys and girls will demolish the entire setup in a couple of minutes.

GUILDS

MATERIALS

Paint and paintbrushes

Markers

Paper

Beeswax

Yarn

White glue

Other craft supplies

INSTRUCTIONS

The Green Ember celebrates art, handi-work, and crafts. Set out a variety of art supplies, and let the children create something beautiful.

PARTY FAVORS

- Small watercolor paint sets to take home

- Rabbit figurines

BY ELSIE IUDICELLO

FIND THE GREEN EMBER

MATERIALS

Notecards with clues

Trinkets to be used as treasures

INSTRUCTIONS

Set up a treasure hunt or small obstacle course using clues from the book or your own imagination.

HEIDI

BY
JOHANNA
SPYRI

Heidi is such a wonderful story and so relatable today. Aren't we all longing for a little more of the countryside and the unadulterated bits of earth still out there? To run with the wind in our hair and have our children grow up free to wander, discover, and explore? I hope you and your little ones enjoy this book!

THE GATHERING

Enjoy an outdoor picnic together. In the invitation, encourage everyone to bring a blanket. Or prepare individual paper bag lunches for the children ahead of time. Add a name tag for a special touch.

FOOD IDEAS

- Mountain spring water
- Fresh goat milk (or regular milk)
- Warm, fresh bread
- Goat cheese
- Apple slices
- Barley soup
- Swiss cheese fondue
- Alpine macaroni (macaroni and cheese with potatoes)
- Spitzbuben (Swiss cookies)

DISCUSSION QUESTIONS

1. Who are the main characters?

2. Where are Heidi's parents?

3. Why does Heidi's Aunt Dete leave her with a grandfather she doesn't even know?

4. Do you think her aunt is acting in Heidi's best interest or her own?

5. What do we know about Heidi's grandfather before she arrives?

6. Where does Heidi sleep at her grandfather's?

7. What is the name of Heidi's friend on the mountain?

8. What does Heidi do all day?

9. Why doesn't Grandfather want Heidi to go to school?

10. How does Heidi help Uncle Alp change?

11. Why does Aunt Dete come to take Heidi to Frankfurt?

12. How long does Heidi think she'll be gone?

13. Why is it hard for Heidi to live in Frankfurt?

14. How does Heidi learn to read?

15. What does everyone think is walking through the house at night? What is it really?

16. What happens to Heidi while living in Frankfurt?

17. What does Heidi do when she returns to the mountains?

18. Which characters are healed when they come to the mountain? How are they healed?

19. Why does Peter act so horribly to Clara when she comes to visit?

20. What happens to Clara when she comes to live on the mountain with Heidi?

21. What are some of the drawbacks of living in the city?

22. What are some benefits of living in the countryside or mountains?

23. How is Heidi a good role model for us?

ACTIVITIES

GOAT TAG

MATERIALS

Ball

INSTRUCTIONS

Use a counting game to select the person who will be "It." Everyone is a goat, but one goat in particular has a ball. The It tries to tag the person with the ball. When the goat is in danger of being tagged, he or she may pass the ball to any other player, in which case the It must try to tag that player instead. If the player holding the ball is touched, he or she becomes the It. If the ball is dropped, the It may capture the ball, and the player who touched it last becomes the It.

WALKING STICKS

Every goatherd or mountain-dweller needs a walking stick, right? Certainly, every adventurer does.

MATERIALS

Scissors

Yarn in various colors

Sticks of suitable size for a child's walking stick

INSTRUCTIONS

Collect an assortment of large sticks of different sizes, suitable for the various children attending. Have the children decorate their walking stick with yarn. They are basically going to "yarn-bomb" a stick, only there's no knitting or crocheting involved, just wrapping.

1. With scissors, cut a piece of yarn of the desired color. Tie one end of the yarn around the stick near the top.

2. Wrap the remaining yarn around the stick, moving downward to cover as much of it as possible. The whole stick doesn't have to be wrapped. In fact, you can encourage the kids to leave parts of their stick bare to expose the wood. Have them see what patterns they can create and envision how they can make theirs stand out.

3. When you reach the end of the yarn, knot the end around the stick.

4. Trim the yarn close to the knot and tuck the loose end under the wrapped portion.

5. Repeat this process with different colors on various parts of the stick.

 **SAFETY TIP**

Using scissors can be dangerous and should be done with adult supervision.

DAISY CHAIN FLOWER CROWNS

It's always fun to make things from pretty blooms. Kids will love making flower crowns—if not for themselves, then for others. I recommend putting one family in charge of foraging (or buying) the wildflowers on the morning of the gathering so they're fresh. If making a crown seems daunting or too long of a process, just make a flower bracelet instead!

MATERIALS

Wildflowers with the longest stems possible

Daisies

Dandelions

INSTRUCTIONS

1. Select three flowers to start, and lay them side by side on a flat surface with the stems positioned vertically and the flower heads at the top.

2. Braid the stems together about an inch.

3. Add a flower by laying it so the stem rests on top of the center stem. Braid another inch, holding the new flower stem together with the center stem.

4. Add another flower in the same way and braid another inch.

5. Continue adding flowers and braiding until the chain is the desired size. Then tuck the ends in near the starter flower head to complete your crown.

PARTY FAVORS

The children will get to take home their handmade flower crowns and walking sticks. If you want to give an additional parting gift to each child, I recommend the following:

- Small mason jars of freshly made goat cheese

- Mini loaves of freshly baked bread wrapped in cheesecloth

- Toblerone bars (delicious Swiss chocolate)

BY AINSLEY ARMENT

THE HOBBIT

BY J. R. R. TOLKIEN

My husband pulled *The Hobbit* out when my oldest child turned six and announced he would start to read it aloud nightly. I now have a fourteen-year-old and three twelve-year-olds, and they are all still drawn to the Shire, Mordor, Rohan, and Rivendell. Tolkien's book encompasses their play and has become the backbone of their childhood together. Sharing this story with others is magical, and I'm so thankful this is now a communal experience with our neighbors and friends.

Tolkien's characters and worlds take on a new meaning each time you read them. They are deep and adventurous. *The Hobbit* has fewer battles than his other volumes and is the perfect way to enter the Shire with younger children.

THE GATHERING

The idea of home is strong throughout *The Hobbit*. Bilbo doesn't want to leave the Shire, his home is comfortable, and he likes everything "just so." For this reason, your home or a familiar neighborhood park is a wonderful place for this book club gathering.

There is no need for much decor, but dressing up does make the event more fun. Ask friends to come in character, and make sure your guests are barefoot to show off their Hobbit feet. If possible, have some props on hand to supplement their costumes:

- Wooden swords
- Capes in earthy colors
- Beards or mustaches
- Flower crowns for elven princesses
- Toy bows and arrows
- Bags for carrying adventuring supplies
- Fur to tape onto guests' Hobbit feet

Another idea is to have name tags and pens near the door when people arrive,

along with a sign that instructs them to come up with elvish or dwarfish names. They can then share the meaning of their names with the group.

FOOD IDEAS

Hobbits love to eat, so food is super important. Specific foods are not mentioned in detail in the book, just the quantity. We thought medieval foods would be appropriate and stuck to meats, fruit, and cheeses that were easy to eat with the hands or pack up for an adventure. For the spiced wine and beer of the novel, we substituted juice and kombucha.

- Whole fruit in a basket
- Cheese tray with veggies and dip
- Chicken or turkey legs
- Kombucha and juice
- Hand pies (sweet or savory)
- Thick slices of sourdough bread
- A variety of cakes

DISCUSSION QUESTIONS

1. What is your favorite character in *The Hobbit*, and why?

2. Describe the Hobbits' homes.

3. What does home mean to a Hobbit?

4. How does Bilbo feel when he leaves the Shire?

5. How is the Shire like your neighborhood? How is it different?

6. Bilbo has to rush to leave for his long journey. Does he pack everything he needs? What would you have taken?

7. What does the Arkenstone represent? Why is it so important?

8. How does Bilbo find the ring?

9. Gollum's personality is basically split in two. How would you describe Gollum, and how does Sméagol differ?

10. How does Gandalf lead even when he isn't present?

11. How do Bilbo and the dwarves escape the Elvenking's palace?

12. The dwarves and elves don't like each other, but they still help each other. How does that work? How do you feel about a grudge going that far back?

13. Where does Bilbo get Sting?

14. Can you describe Smaug's personality or character? How did Smaug get his treasure?

15. Bilbo and the adventurers are selective about what they take from Smaug. Why are their trophies significant?

ACTIVITIES

MAKE THE MARK ON THE HOBBIT DOOR

MATERIALS

Paper (enough to cover the door)
Tape
Door
Marker
Blindfold

INSTRUCTIONS

With paper and tape, cover as much of the door as your kids can reach. Give one of the children a marker and blindfold them. Much like Pin the Tail on the Donkey, have

the child try to make a mark on the middle of the paper-covered door and see how close they get. You could also play Pin the Tail on Smaug in the same fashion.

DRAGON ARCHERY

MATERIALS

Large picture of a dragon

Tape or glue

Cardboard box (medium to large size)

Toy bow and arrow

INSTRUCTIONS

Set up the target by affixing the dragon image on the side of the cardboard box. Attach it firmly enough that it stays in place when hit. Line up the kids and have them stand an appropriate distance away from the box. Give the first kid in line the bow and arrow and instruct them to shoot at the dragon. Give each kid three tries to hit the dragon. If you'd like to turn it into a competition, you can assign point values to different parts of the dragon (such as 5 points for hitting the belly, 10 points for the tail, 15 points for the head). The first kid to reach a predetermined number wins.

PAINT YOUR OWN ARKENSTONE

MATERIALS

Paint

Paintbrushes

Medium-size rocks (one per child)

INSTRUCTIONS

Have the children use paint to decorate rocks like the Arkenstone for the perfect take-home memory.

WHERE IS BILBO?

MATERIALS

Plastic ring

INSTRUCTIONS

Designate one child as "Bilbo," who vanishes when he puts on the ring. Have all the other children close their eyes, then have Bilbo put on the ring and hide. See if the other children can find Bilbo using senses other than sight.

WHO HAS THE RING?

MATERIALS

Plastic ring

INSTRUCTIONS

In this version of the game Heads Up, Seven Up (search online for instructions as needed), the players pass the ring around and try to deceive the child serving as "It."

CREATE YOUR OWN HOBBIT HOLE

MATERIALS

Play-Doh

INSTRUCTIONS

Have the children use Play-Doh or clay to create their own Hobbit hole in the Shire, complete with a round doorway.

RIDDLE TIME

"What has roots as nobody sees, is taller than the trees, up, up it goes, and yet never grows?" Gollum asks.

MATERIALS

Riddles from a book or online

INSTRUCTIONS

Have your guests take turns asking silly riddles and working out the answers together.

PARTY FAVORS

Children will take home the Arkenstone and the Hobbit hole they made at the party. Here are some additional ideas:

- Elven ciphers using runes from the book matched with the English alphabet (this is a fun way to create a secret message to thank your guests for coming)

- Plastic jewels in small muslin bags for Smaug's treasure

- Plastic rings

BY BRIT CHAMBERS

ISLAND OF THE BLUE DOLPHINS

BY SCOTT O'DELL

sland of the Blue Dolphins is a heavy book. Characters die, most of a village is massacred, the heroine is abandoned and experiences years of isolation on an island in the Pacific, and there is even an earthquake and a tsunami to overcome! I cracked open the book to read aloud during lunch one day, wondering where such depth would take us. When I finished reading the last sentence aloud, I asked my children what they thought the tale was about. Their responses floored me:

- "It's a beautiful story about making a full life out of loneliness."

- "It's a story about survival, not just life survival but heart survival, like how she was always creating beautiful things instead of giving up."

- "It's a story about forgiveness and love between a girl and a dog."

Literature is a beautiful way to help our children emotionally sort out the world around them. Stories like *Island of the Blue Dolphins* are vital during our children's growing years. They allow children to experience human brokenness safely from the harbor of their home. Tucked in bed or curled against their parent's side, they can experience characters who suffer, adapt, grow, and triumph in a variety of settings and situations.

Children absorb these triumphs into their hearts and minds, a deposit in their reservoirs of truth, beauty, and goodness. We cannot shield them from the hard edges of the world forever, but we can walk beside them along the precipice of raw human experience in the pages of a worthy book as they hunt for words to name their emotions and live them out.

THE GATHERING

Here are some locations to consider for your book club:

- A beach or nearby body of water
- A cave or other interesting rock formation
- A backyard packed with kiddie pools and tents
- A home filled with love

FOOD IDEAS

- Dried fruit
- Seaweed
- Coconut water
- Trail mix

DISCUSSION QUESTIONS

1. Describe an animal encounter that Karana experiences. What lessons does she learn from it? Have you ever learned a lesson from nature?

2. What are some of the cultural traditions that Karana integrates into her new solitary life once her community is gone? What are some traditions she abandoned? Are there any special traditions in your home that you would like to take with you one day?

3. Why does Karana leave the island, and what brings her back? Try to recall her thought process as she rows farther and farther out to sea.

4. Karana faces many losses and changes throughout the book. What did you learn about her character through her responses to difficult moments?

5. What place do art and creativity have in Karana's life? How do they affect her daily life?

6. What kinds of friendships does Karana have once she is left alone on the island? What needed to happen before those friendships could come about?

7. If you were alone on an island, would you do anything the way Karana did? What sorts of things would you do differently?

8. How do Karana's thoughts and practices regarding animals change over the course of the book? What causes the change?

ACTIVITIES

MAKE NECKLACES

MATERIALS

String or twine (one for each child)

Beads

Clasps (optional)

INSTRUCTIONS

Give each child a piece of string and some beads and let them string their own beautiful necklace. Cut the string to each child's size. Have them knot the string, or help them put a clasp on the necklace so they can wear it home if they want.

 SAFETY TIP

Using scissors can be dangerous and should be done with adult supervision.

OTTERS VS. DOLPHINS GROUP TAG

INSTRUCTIONS

In a large outdoor space, organize a game of group tag. Split the kids into two groups—otters and dolphins—then let them have fun running around.

BUILD A SHELTER FORT

MATERIALS

Blankets, pillows, and sheets if inside

Branches, rocks, and beach towels if outside

INSTRUCTIONS

Build a shelter by making a fort either indoors or outdoors. Then, equip it for survival, bringing in any items you might need if you were stranded on an island.

PARTY FAVORS

- Shell necklaces (either handmade or inexpensive store-bought ones)
- Muslin bags of seashells

BY ELSIE IUDICELLO

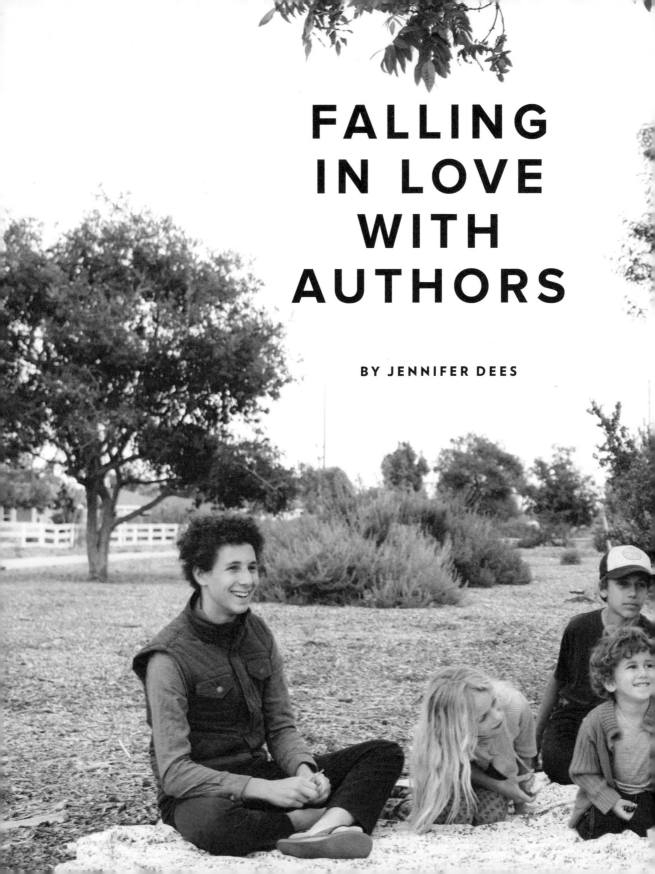

FALLING IN LOVE WITH AUTHORS

BY JENNIFER DEES

My family chose the novel *White Fang* to read with our book club. Author Jack London describes in detail the world from the point of view of a wolf, allowing readers to use their imagination and share in the adventure. Through this book, he makes the Alaska of a bygone era come alive.

The more my kids and I researched the author, the more fascinated we became with him. London is largely a forgotten writer today. His name is well known, but many avid readers I ask have not read him. In his own time, the early 1900s, he was one of the most famous American writers. He was so well known that President Theodore Roosevelt commented publicly on his work, even getting upset that London wrote of a lynx defeating a wolf in *White Fang*, a scenario that Roosevelt found unrealistic.

You can bring an author into your children's life in a way that lodges in their heart forever. Here are some ways to do so:

- Find a story that they love, and research the author's life. Ask questions such as these: Where did the inspiration for this story come from? Did the author travel and have unique experiences? How did the author's experiences find their way into the story?

- Start a book club. Have the children share their favorite sections of the story and ask each other questions such as: Why do you like this book? What do you think the author wanted us to think of the characters?

- Find an audio version of the book recorded by a good narrator whose voice fits the style of the book. We love John Lee's reading of *White Fang* and *The Call of the Wild*.

- Dig deeper into an author's background by visiting a museum with artifacts from his or her life. You may be able to visit the author's birthplace too. My kids' book club visited the Huntington Library in Pasadena, California, where an original manuscript of *White Fang* is on display, as well as notes written by London.

A well-written story is timeless. We were able to savor our time learning with Jack London, and through his stories, we were given a glimpse into the harsh Alaska wilderness. His stories still tell us something of humanity's interaction with animals, in all its beauty and sometimes cruelty. London's writing reflected his life and passions, and in this way, we became acquainted with a man who has passed from this earth but who is still very much alive through his words.

"Unlike television, reading does not swallow the senses or dictate thought. Reading stimulates the ecology of the imagination. Can you remember the wonder you felt when first reading *The Jungle Book* or *Tom Sawyer* or *Huckleberry Finn*? Kipling's world within a world, Twain's slow river, the feel of freedom and sand on the secret island, and in the depths of the cave?"

—Richard Louv

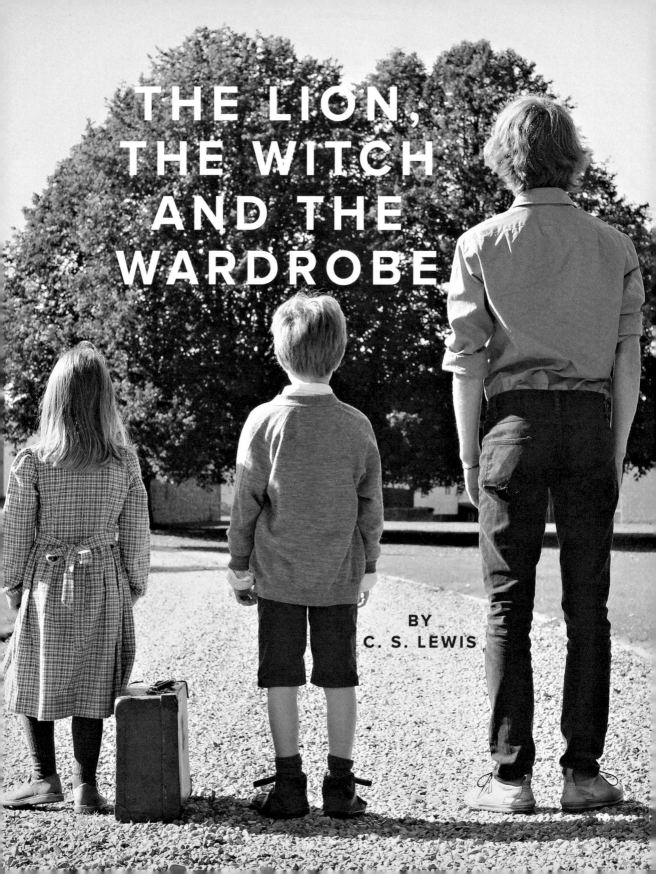

THE LION, THE WITCH AND THE WARDROBE

BY
C. S. LEWIS

read *The Lion, the Witch and the Wardrobe* when I was about ten. It transported me to a world of fantasy and excitement, and I couldn't put it down. When I took my own children out to recreate some of the scenes in the story through pictures, the book came alive for me all over again!

I stopped more than once to see the world through their eyes, noticing how time stands still when you live in the moment, in your imagination—something the book handles brilliantly with years going by in Narnia, yet no time at all in reality. Most important, I introduced my two younger children to a series of books about adventure, about imagination, and, above all, about what is possible if you really believe in yourself.

THE GATHERING

You can host this book club gathering at home, transforming your home into your own magic portal to Narnia. For decor, think white: "always winter, never Christmas." I recommend using handmade paper snowflake garlands, white linens, tree branches covered in faux snow, and of course twinkle lights. Turn your front door into a wardrobe entrance by covering it with brown paper. Hang some faux fur coats and a lantern inside. Cast the vision for the theme and even invite the children to come dressed in character (for example, mid-century skirts and sweaters or button-down shirts and suspenders).

FOOD IDEAS

A few food ideas include Turkish delight and hot cocoa, which are the two things that led to Edmund's fall. You could also set up a "Mr. Tumnus's Tea Table" and an "Eternal Winter" cookie-decorating station.

The meal that the four children share at the Beavers' home is good and simple to replicate for a cozy Narnia experience: fried trout, boiled potatoes, warm bread with deep yellow butter, and creamy milk. For dessert, the characters enjoy a "great and gloriously sticky marmalade roll, steaming hot," and cups of tea.

If you have a lot of younger kids or time restraints, instead offer premade sandwiches wrapped in brown paper and tied up with string.

DISCUSSION QUESTIONS

1. Who are the main characters in the book?

2. Why do the children have to leave London?

3. Who is the first to discover Narnia? And how do they do it?

4. What curse is Narnia under?

5. Why do you think Lucy cries when her siblings don't believe her story?

6. What does the White Witch make for Edmund from the snow? Why doesn't he want Peter and Susan to know?

7. Where do the four children go first when they all get to Narnia?

8. What landmark do the children use to find their way home?

9. Who helps the children when they discover Mr. Tumnus is in trouble?

10. Mr. Beaver says of Aslan, "'Course he isn't safe. But he's good." What does he mean?

11. What happened to those who went against the White Witch?

12. Why does Father Christmas give the children weapons?

13. What is the price that needs to be paid for Edmund's betrayal?

14. Why does the White Witch want to kill Edmund?

15. What deal does Aslan strike with the White Witch?

16. Who follows Aslan on the night he is killed? How did you feel when Aslan was killed?

17. What does Aslan do when he comes back to life?

18. How does Aslan bring those turned to stone back to life?

19. How did you feel when the children went back into the wardrobe to return to the real world?

20. Who does Aslan represent? List some of his character traits.

ACTIVITIES

NARNIA SNOW GLOBES

MATERIALS

Small mason jars or jelly jars with lids (one for each child)

Water-resistant glue

Bag of fake snow

White glitter

Glycerin

Water

Small figurines like lampposts, pine trees, or animals

INSTRUCTIONS

1. Glue a figurine (a lamppost, a tree, or an animal) to the inside of the lid.

2. Add a pinch of glitter and fake snow to the jar.

3. Fill the jar three-quarters of the way to the top with water.

4. Add a dash of glycerin, which helps the glitter fall slowly. Don't add too much, or the snow will stick to the jar.

5. Glue the lid to keep it secure and close the jar.

6. Flip the jar over, and let it snow!

ETERNAL WINTER COOKIE-DECORATING STATION

MATERIALS

Icing

Bowls of various toppings, like sprinkles and tiny candy snowflakes

Plastic knives and spoons

Paper plates

Sugar cookies (a few for each child)

INSTRUCTIONS

Set out the icing, toppings, and plastic utensils on a table. Give each child a paper plate and a few cookies. I recommend having the kids sit around the table, as opposed

to forming an assembly line, so they can settle in and get creative with their decorations. Depending on the number of children, you will most likely need to have both the icing and decorating stations going simultaneously.

PARTY FAVORS

Fill a sack with special gifts for each child. You could create a magical healing cordial, like the one Lucy was given, by collecting small vials and filling them with water and a few drops of essential oils. Any small token would be a wonderful surprise and delight, especially if you have Father Christmas visit to distribute the gifts in his white beard and long red robe.

BY ALI DOVER

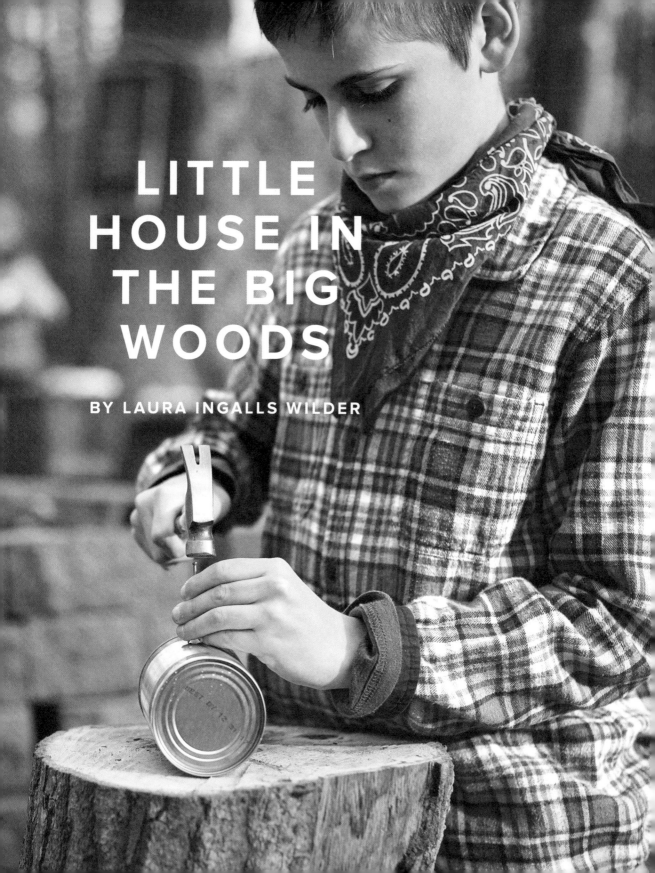

LITTLE HOUSE IN THE BIG WOODS

BY LAURA INGALLS WILDER

Laura Ingalls Wilder's beloved Little House series has enthralled generations who agree that "home is the nicest word there is." Set in the 1870s, *Little House in the Big Woods* tells the heartwarming story of a young pioneer girl who lives with her family in a log cabin in the woods of Wisconsin.

The book's timeless themes of home and family, nature, courage, and frontier life resonate with families today—and especially with my own as we've recently moved to our very own "house in the big woods." This glimpse into life in a slower era inspires me to step back from the hustle and bustle of the day-to-day and encourages my family to unplug, slow down, and enjoy the woods and quiet that surround us.

THE GATHERING

Host this book club at home. You could also pair it with a movie night and settle in to watch the television show *Little House on the Prairie* afterward. To evoke the feel of Laura Ingalls's quaint woodland home, ask the kids to dress up in "pioneer" clothing: bonnets and skirts or handkerchiefs and plaid shirts. Playing "fiddling"

music in the background adds an authentic touch. Pioneer decorations are easy to create if you want a more festive event. You can use materials you already have on hand or can find easily at a thrift store. We incorporated the following in our decor:

- A vintage quilt hung over a makeshift clothesline
- Kraft paper coverings for tables
- Slate chalkboards for labeling foods and for decor
- Galvanized washtubs and wooden crates for use as containers and for decor
- Mason jars or milk bottle jars for drinking
- Jute twine
- Pine cones, acorns, and other natural woodland items
- Wooden benches made from tree stumps and boards

FOOD IDEAS

Food plays a central role in Laura's story. From winter storage to harvest time, the Ingalls's lives revolve around food preparation throughout the seasons. This party

menu requires little preparation but reminds young readers of the foods that pioneers prepared.

- "Smokehouse" ham and cheese roll-ups (deli ham and cheese sticks sealed with toothpicks)
- Johnnycake (skillet cornbread) topped with homemade butter from the activity
- Popcorn and apple bar
- Pretzels and nut or seed butter for building log cabins
- Laura's old-fashioned lemonade (can be purchased and garnished with fresh lemons)
- Maple snow candy

DISCUSSION QUESTIONS

1. Who is your favorite character? Do you have anything in common with them?

2. Is there a particular part of the book you enjoyed (or disliked) more than the rest?

3. What are Laura and Mary's evenings like?

4. Think about the stories that Pa tells in the book. Which is your favorite?

5. What are some of the chores that Laura and Mary have to do?

6. What are some of the challenges Laura's family faces as pioneers?

7. How do they overcome those challenges?

8. What scary situations do the characters face? How do they show bravery?

9. How does the Ingalls family prepare for winter?

10. What is the most interesting food the family prepares or harvests?

11. What do you think was the most interesting aspect of pioneer life?

12. How was Laura's life in the late 1800s different from your life today?

13. What is "sugar snow," and what does it mean for the Ingalls?

14. Are there any foods mentioned in the book that you would like to try?

15. How does Laura's family celebrate Christmas?

ACTIVITIES

HOMEMADE BUTTER

Laura's family makes homemade butter in a churn, but it's easy to make in small jars too. This is a favorite activity that uses a lot of kid energy!

MATERIALS

Heavy whipping cream

Small jars with lids (baby food jars work great)

INSTRUCTIONS

Fill the jars halfway with heavy whipping cream, and shake, shake, and shake some more. Shake until the whey separates from the butterfat and small balls of butter form. It can take 15 to 20 minutes of shaking to turn whipping cream into butter, so have the children take turns! The jars can be set down to rest between shaking.

Once the butter is solid, place it on a clean tea towel, and squeeze out the excess liquid. Place the butter in a container, and save it to spread on the johnnycake.

DROP THE CLOTHESPIN

This is a fun pioneer game that uses clothespins like the ones Laura's family used to dry their wash.

MATERIALS

Glass milk bottles or other containers with a narrow opening (1 per child)

Wooden clothespins without springs (5 per child)

INSTRUCTIONS

1. Line the kids up in a row and place a glass milk bottle on the ground in front of each one. Give each child five clothespins.

2. The children try to drop their clothespins into the bottle from a standing position.

3. The person who gets the most clothespins in the bottle wins. Or you can decide that the first person to drop a clothespin into a bottle is the winner.

TIN LANTERNS

This is a beautiful craft that makes a fun keepsake as well. **NOTE:** This activity requires supervision and is best suited for older children, but younger children can participate with an adult's help.

MATERIALS

Hammers

Small sharp nails

Tin cans (rinsed, labels and lids removed)

Craft wire or jute string

Small tea-light candles or battery-operated candles

INSTRUCTIONS

1. Using a hammer and a nail, puncture a pattern into a tin can.

2. Use craft wire or jute string to create a handle for the lantern.

3. Place a tea-light candle inside the can, and watch your lanterns shine bright in the evening. Use a battery-operated candle for young children.

BY STEPHANIE BEATY

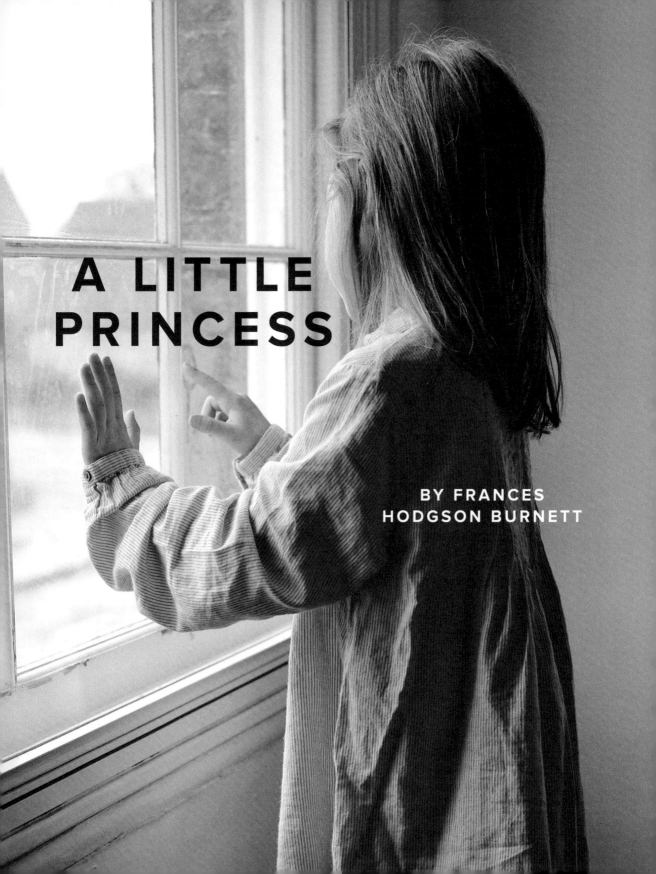

A LITTLE PRINCESS

BY FRANCES
HODGSON BURNETT

While reading *A Little Princess* with my children, I couldn't help but think of my mother, who grew up in the 1950s. Her mother worked several jobs in a small town on the Jersey Shore. My mom was a sickly child and had an abusive, alcoholic stepfather. She took on a lot of the household chores and often worked with her mother setting up banquets at a fancy hotel before school.

But it wasn't the hardships faced by Sara Crewe, the protagonist in *A Little Princess*, that reminded me most of my mother. It was her imagination. When my mother was a little girl, she loved to dress up like a princess. She would put on her mother's long fancy gloves, jewelry, and dresses. She didn't just pretend she was a princess; she actually *believed* she was a princess. She explained, "I imagined I had been born a princess, misplaced in a common family, and no one understood. But I couldn't change who I was born to be." My mother wasn't haughty. In fact, she was the kindest, most loving person I've ever known. But she used her imagination to find happiness in spite of her difficult circumstances, just like Sara Crewe.

THE GATHERING

A Little Princess takes place at a boarding school in London, but the real magic happens in Sara Crewe's damp and dim attic, which became the focus of our book club setting. Host your book club in your home, at a church, or in a community center. If you have an attic or a space that could be transformed to look like a dim attic, even better! This is a good book club to have in the colder months when you can be inside with a warm fire.

Invite the children to come dressed in character (Victorian-era suits and hats or dresses with big bows in the hair). Find some Indian fabrics, if possible, and use them as tablecloths, wall hangings, or sofa coverings. Create a suitable ambience by using only natural light with a few candles burning (if age appropriate) and have a nice warm fire going.

FOOD IDEAS

Set up an English tea table with a carafe of hot water, various teas, cream, and sugar cubes. Use a tiered plate or cupcake holder for an array of scones and other pastries.

- Heart-shaped sandwiches (create with a cookie cutter)
- Fruit and vegetable kabobs
- Mini quiches
- Scones
- Muffins

DISCUSSION QUESTIONS

1. Who are the main characters in *A Little Princess*?

2. Are the characters likable? Which characters would you like to be friends with in real life?

3. What do the other girls enjoy listening to Sara do?

4. What makes Sara a likable character?

5. Where does Sara live before going to Miss Minchin's school in London?

6. Why do you think Lavinia is so mean to Sara?

7. Why do the other girls call Sara a little princess?

8. What happens to Sara when her father dies?

9. Who is still kind to Sara and visits her at night?

10. Sara uses her imagination to keep strong during this difficult time. Have you ever used your imagination in this way?

11. One time when Sara is very hungry, she finds a coin and buys some rolls. Then she sees a beggar girl and gives them away. Why does Sara give her rolls to the girl, even though she is hungry?

12. The lady at the bakery is moved to show kindness herself when she sees what Sara does. Have you ever been in a situation where one person's kindness caused someone else to act kindly?

13. Is Sara a leader? Why or why not? If so, is she a good leader?

14. Is Lavinia a leader? Why or why not? If so, is she a good leader?

15. What does it mean to Sara to be a princess?

16. What does it mean to Lavinia to be a princess?

17. What kind of creature sneaks into Sara's room? Who comes to retrieve it?

18. What do you think is the climax of the story of *A Little Princess*?

19. How does Sara end up in Mr. Carrisford's home?

20. How does Sara's life change during her visit with Mr. Carrisford?

21. What role does imagination play in this story?

ACTIVITIES

KINDNESS JARS

Talk with the children about how Sara shows kindness to others and how it causes others to show kindness themselves. Remind them that sometimes people don't repay kindness shown to them, and that's okay. Encourage the children to keep their kindness jar going after the first week, even if they only draw one slip of paper on Saturdays.

MATERIALS

Mason jars (have children bring their own)

Glue

Scraps of fabric

Yarn or twine

Strips of paper (seven for each child)

Pens and pencils

INSTRUCTIONS

1. Have the children decorate their jars by gluing scraps of pretty fabric to them and then tying some yarn around the top.

2. Give each child seven strips of paper. Have the children write on each strip one act of kindness that they could do for others (siblings, friends, parents, strangers, etc.).

3. Have them put the papers in the jar, and tell them that they can draw one every day to fulfill over the next week.

STICK CROWNS

This simple crown craft will appeal to everyone.

MATERIALS

Measuring tape

Scissors

Paper grocery bags

Hot glue gun

Sticks and twigs

Crayons

Flowers (real or fake)

Fake jewels (optional)

Hole punch

Yarn or twine

INSTRUCTIONS

1. Measure the child's head.

2. From the grocery bags, cut two strips of paper, each about 2 inches wide and 2 inches shorter in length than the measurement from step 1.

3. Lay down one strip horizontally and use a hot glue gun to create two vertical rows of glue in the center of the paper.

4. Quickly lay down five or six sticks side by side on the hot glue.

5. Make two more rows of glue, this time going from end to end, and adhere the second strip of paper to the first (the sticks will be sandwiched in between).

6. When the glue dries, the children can decorate the outside of the paper with crayons and adhere the flowers or jewels.

7. Finally, punch a hole in both ends of the joined strips, and use a piece of yarn to tie the crown onto the child's head.

 SAFETY TIP

Using hot glue and scissors can be dangerous and should be done with adult supervision.

BY AINSLEY ARMENT

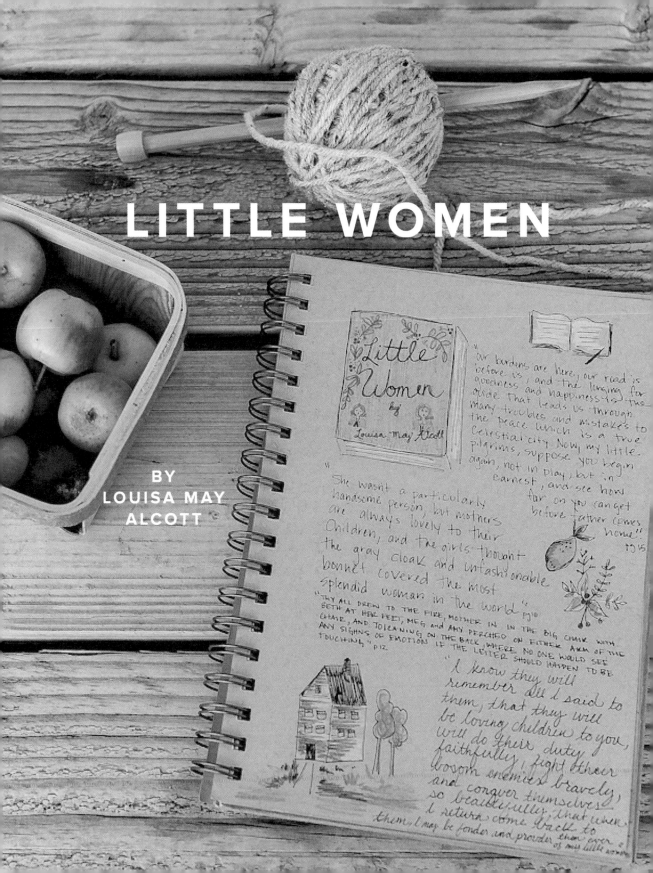

LITTLE WOMEN

BY
LOUISA MAY
ALCOTT

ot many books have had quite the impact on my family as this book. *Little Women* is a lovely coming-of-age story that Louisa May Alcott based on her own life. It is filled with the rich values of family, loyalty, patience, generosity, modesty, and hard work. And although this book is about four sisters, you can be sure that everyone will enjoy it.

THE GATHERING

There are endless options for where to host your book club. The ideal location depends on a few factors, such as how large your group is, what the weather is like, and how much prep work you want to do. Here are a few ideas:

- A room with a fireplace where you can cozy up like the March sisters in the first chapter
- A Colonial-style house, like the March sisters' New England home
- A lake or seaside site where you can have a simple picnic or collect shells like Jo and Beth

To decorate, you can ask each child to bring trinkets from home that remind them of their favorite characters. Lay them out on a table. These items can be turned into a game as well by having everyone guess to which characters the items belong. Here are a few ideas:

- Piano music and seashells for Beth
- Books for Jo
- Gloves for Meg

- Art supplies for Amy
- Old war letters for Mr. March
- Glasses or a pair of slippers for Mr. Laurence

DISCUSSION QUESTIONS

1. In the first chapter, the girls find out they have no money for Christmas gifts. How do they react to this? Do you think you would have reacted the same way?

2. Who is your favorite character, and why?

3. What important lesson do the girls learn from all play and no work?

4. What is your favorite part of the book? What is your least favorite?

5. What is Jo's greatest honor?

6. Use one word each to describe Meg, Jo, Beth, and Amy.

7. Were you upset that Laurie marries Amy instead of Jo? How are they a better match?

8. Describe Professor Bhaer. What do you think of him?

9. Would you recommend *Little Women* to a friend? Why or why not?

10. Do you think this book is outdated, or is it still relevant to current times?

11. Do you like how the book ends? Why or why not?

RIGMAROLE

Gathering kids together to tell a silly story can be a lot of fun. In the book, Miss Kate explains: "One person begins a story, any nonsense you like, and tells as long as he pleases, only taking care to stop short at some exciting point, when the next takes it up and does the same. It's very funny when well done and makes a perfect jumble of tragical comical stuff to laugh over."

INSTRUCTIONS

Have the children sit in a circle. Once child starts telling a story, and the next child adds to it. This continues all around the circle until the last child finishes the story. The kids will love this fun and engaging activity of storytelling, if they can finish for all the giggling.

 SAFETY TIP

Using knives can be dangerous and should be done with adult supervision.

AMY'S PICKLED LIMES

This activity is based on Amy's limes: "It's nothing but limes now, for everyone is sucking them in their desks at school time, and trading them off for pencils, bead rings, or paper dolls at recess."

INGREDIENTS

8 limes

Salt

INSTRUCTIONS

1. Rinse the limes and cut off their ends.

2. Slit a lengthwise "X" onto each of the limes, just breaking the skin.

3. Pack the salt into the slits.

4. Place the limes in a jar and seal it.

5. After 12 hours, press the limes firmly in the jar until they are submerged into the juice.

6. Chill the limes in the refrigerator for a month before eating.

BY JENNIFER NARAKI

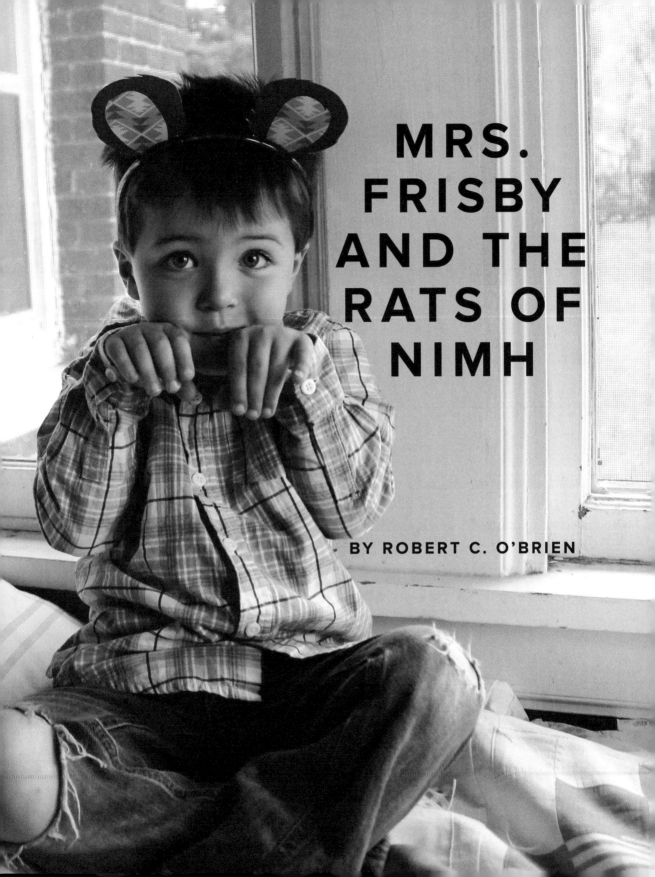

MRS. FRISBY AND THE RATS OF NIMH

BY ROBERT C. O'BRIEN

Since childhood, I've had an irrational fear of small furry rodents. It's ironic, then, that several of my favorite books feature such creatures as main characters—characters that have become, surprisingly, beloved and heroic examples. They were the comrades of my childhood and are now the same to my children.

Mrs. Frisby and the Rats of NIMH, winner of the 1972 Newbery Medal, tells the tale of a widowed field mouse, Mrs. Frisby, who finds her family in desperate danger and seeks the aid of a local colony of uniquely intelligent rats. The rats themselves share an incredible and intriguing history, and Mrs. Frisby soon finds herself caught up in adventure, daring acts, and strong kinship with the rats.

THE GATHERING

Most of the story takes place on the Fitzgibbons' farm, so hosting your book club at a rural site would work well. If a barnyard or farm is not available, try setting up in or near a garden, since this is where the Frisby family lives and works to survive the coming of the dreaded plow.

Rosebushes would be a perfect nod to the rosebush that hides the entrance and exit of the rats' nest. A field trip to a laboratory might be an interesting enrichment exercise sometime after the book club.

Here are some ideas for decoration:

- Burlap or old quilts to cover the tables
- Moss, rocks, and pieces of wood for natural touches
- Garden tools
- Seed packets
- Paper cutouts of the animals in the story (we chose Nicodemus the rat, Mr. Ages the white mouse, Mrs. Frisby the field mouse, and Jeremy the crow)
- Wooden or pottery dishes in complementary colors
- Terra-cotta pots
- A cinder block like the one in which the Frisbys make their home
- A potted dwarf rosebush in bloom or fresh-cut (or silk) roses in a rustic container

FOOD IDEAS

We thought like mice and laid out a spread fit for a rodent king. Ask each family or book club attendee to bring an ingredient for trail mix, a garden vegetable cut into finger-food size, and a type of cheese.

Here are some ideas for what to prepare:

- **BUILD YOUR OWN TRAIL-MIX BAR:** Set out the ingredients in small terra-cotta pots and lay out a mini gardening trowel to use as a serving scoop. The ingredients can include nuts, coconut chips, dried fruit pieces, chocolate-coated candies, pretzel "twigs," granola, and sunflower seeds. Add small muslin or burlap cinch-top bags if you would like to send the individualized mixes home as favors. It's fun to see what everyone likes in their mix, and you can talk about how the rats of NIMH haul grain and seeds to their new home.

- **CHEESE BOARD:** Add little labels near each cheese to announce the type. Paper flags on toothpicks work great poked into the main block of each cheese. Pre-cut the cheese into bite-size pieces, especially if you have a lot of younger children attending who might not be able to handle a cheese knife.

- **FRESH GARDEN VEGETABLE PLATTER:** A yummy balance for the sweet treats!

- **"DIRT" CAKE:** This is a delightful addition to the garden theme, especially when presented in a terra-cotta pot and dished up with a trowel. Recipes are readily available online. We left off the traditional gummy worms and topped our cake with paper rodent cutouts attached to popsicle sticks instead.

DISCUSSION QUESTIONS

1. Why are Mrs. Frisby's family and home in danger?

2. Who would you talk to if your home or family were in danger?

3. What does the phrase "We all help each other against the cat" mean to you?

4. Discuss how it might feel to be a mouse visiting an owl for advice. How would you feel if you had to ask for help from the mysterious rats under the rosebush?

5. How was Jonathan a friend to the rats?

6. Many characters in this book exemplify bravery. Can you give an example?

7. Put yourself in the place of Dr. Schultz. How might you argue that your experiments are worthwhile?

8. Put yourself in the place of the rats of NIMH. How might you argue that you should be free?

9. What does the phrase "discontent settled upon us like some creeping disease" mean to you? Have you ever felt discontent? What changed? What makes you feel content?

10. Nicodemus presents some big questions about what it means to be truly free and keep making progress as a civilization. Share your thoughts about this line: "We did not have enough work to do because a thief's life is always based on somebody else's work." How can you understand Nicodemus's point of view?

11. How does Jenner feel about The Plan? Can you understand how he feels? Share how you might feel if you were him.

ACTIVITIES

THE NIMH NAME GAME

MATERIALS

Sticky notes (one for each child)

Pen or pencil

INSTRUCTIONS

This game can be played a couple of ways, depending on the size of your group.

FOR A LARGER GROUP: Write the name of a different animal from the book on each sticky note, and attach one to each child's forehead. The child should not see the name beforehand or be told what it says. The goal for each player is to figure out who they are by walking around and asking the other players yes or no questions to deduce the name affixed to their head. Continue until everyone knows who they are.

FOR A SMALLER GROUP: Start out the same, but instead of walking around asking other players, have the children pair off and take turns asking their partner questions until one person guesses their own name correctly. Labels could refer to general species (owl, rat, crow, etc.) or to actual character names for added difficulty.

MOUSEY EARS CRAFT

MATERIALS

Scissors

Cardstock in neutral colors, like white, gray, and brown

Patterned paper for inner ear (optional)

Hot glue gun

Plastic headbands in neutral colors

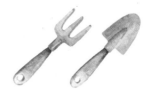

INSTRUCTIONS

1. Cut out a mouse ear shape from the cardstock and use it as a stencil for a second ear of the same size and shape. Repeat with the patterned paper to create two smaller pieces for the inner ear, if desired. **NOTE:** For younger children, cut out a template from lightweight cardboard for them to trace, and have an adult handy to use the hot glue gun.

2. Glue the inner ear to the outer ear, then glue both ears to a headband.

 **SAFETY TIP**

Using hot glue and scissors can be dangerous and should be done with adult supervision.

PARTY FAVORS

• Packets of garden seeds

• Small fuzzy, plastic, or wooden toy mice, rats, or other woodland creatures mentioned in the story

• Small garden tools

• Small notebooks and twig pencils that the children can use for planning their own future home or adventure

BY RAIMIE HARRISON

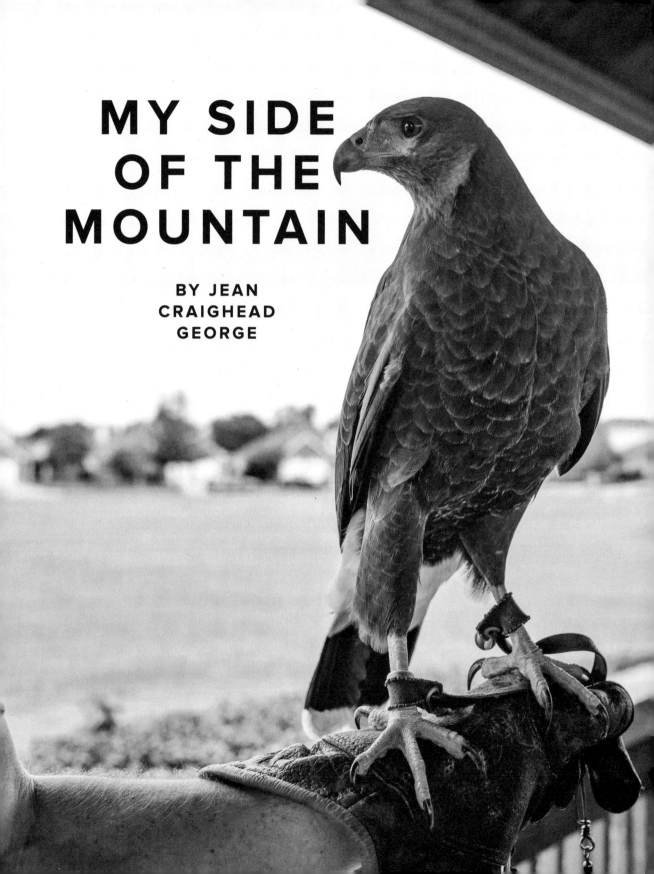

MY SIDE OF THE MOUNTAIN

BY JEAN CRAIGHEAD GEORGE

nhance your child's dream of living out in the wild with *My Side of the Mountain*. As we follow the adventure of Sam Gribley, a young boy who dreams of living off the land in the Catskill Mountains, we learn not only of a boy's love of nature but also sound practical advice. My son raced through this book, eager to follow the grand adventure, and now uses his newfound knowledge when we go hiking and camping. What makes this wilderness book unique are the countless ways kids can apply Sam's experiences to their lives. Although this book is a novel, the author provides detailed accounts of Sam's diet, clothes, habitat, and struggles throughout the different seasons. If you enjoy this book, keep reading! There are more books in the series, including *On the Far Side of the Mountain* and *Frightful's Mountain*.

THE GATHERING

If you are fortunate enough to live near a mountain range, your location for hosting this book club will be obvious: the mountains make a perfect backdrop to discuss, play, and feast. And if you don't live near the mountains, pick a local outdoor venue, such as a nature center or wildlife preserve, where the children can make believe they are living in the wild as they delve into the world of Sam Gribley.

In the book, Sam lives inside an oak tree near a stream, so consider setting up where children can build forts or fish, building the cave dwelling of their dreams and splashing in the water.

Dress up your food table with items from Sam's tree cave: a hand-drawn tally calendar, a nature-inspired journal, a wooden whistle or flute, acorns, and local flowers. Additionally, you can decorate with printouts of the common plants from the book (oak trees, cattails, violet bulbs, wild onions, and apple trees) and bring stuffed animals, such as a peregrine falcon, raccoon, and weasel.

FOOD IDEAS

Sam loves to make feasts for his guests and quickly learns how to live off the land by watching the animals that live in the mountains. Your group could go all out and attempt to re-create some of Sam's favorite dishes, including using acorn powder for pancakes and fresh berries for jam. Here are a few other ideas:

- Cooked fish
- Walnuts (or other nuts) and seeds
- Apples
- Tea
- Venison (or perhaps beef jerky)

DISCUSSION QUESTIONS

1. Why does Sam Gribley want to live in the mountains?

2. How do you think you would manage living in the forest?

3. Living in the forest was Sam's dream. If you could live anywhere, where would it be, and why?

4. What does Sam discover how to do first? Why is this so important?

5. What practical tips can we learn from Sam's adventures?

6. What would be the hardest part of living in the wild for you? What is Sam's biggest challenge?

7. Discuss your favorite one of Sam's animal companions. Why is it your favorite?

8. Discuss your favorite one of Sam's human companions. Why are they your favorite?

9. Why do you think the newspaper reporters and others are so focused on discovering Sam?

10. What did you anticipate when Sam's father came to visit? How would your parent(s) react if they found you living in a tree in the mountain?

11. Discuss the following quotation from the book: "You can't live in America today and be quietly different."

12. What was your reaction when Sam's family comes to live with him at the end of the book?

ACTIVITIES

Your book club could include a variety of outdoor activities.

- **LEARN TO BUILD A FIRE:** If no one in your group has experience with starting fires, invite a scout leader to teach you. Discuss fire safety as well as different types of outdoor fires. Consider using flint and steel or natural materials to start your fire.

- **GO FISHING:** Whether you meet at a large lake or a small stream, use store-bought fishing poles or handmade rods, fishing is a fun activity that can be enhanced by discussing the different types of fish native to your area.

- **FORAGE FOR YOUR SNACK:** So much of nature truly can be eaten. Consider inviting a foraging expert to give a talk.

- **MAKE A MAP:** Discuss how maps are created and map out a small section of the area. Include markers such as trees, picnic benches, and other important landmarks.

- **DISCOVER BIRDS OF PREY**: Bring in a wildlife expert, such as a falconer, to truly bring the book to life. If an expert is not available, keep your eyes open. Many areas have hawks or other birds of prey that can give children a sense of who kept Sam company for all those months.

- **HAND-SEW A POUCH**: Sew together small fabric scraps or lightweight leather to create a bag or pouch for holding treasures your kids find in nature.

PARTY FAVORS

Send the children home with some unique goodies to help them remember the day and to enhance their outdoor activities:

- Wooden whistles
- Journals made from natural materials
- Fire-starter kits for older children

BY DANA NOWELL

COLLABORATING WITH GREAT AUTHORS

BY SHARON MCKEEMAN

A few months ago, after reading with my boys one of our favorite books, *Tom Sawyer*, we read Twain's newest book, *The Purloining of Prince Oleomargarine*. Published in 2017, it is based on sixteen pages of handwritten notes that Twain jotted down about a particularly well-received bedtime story he told his girls.

We can all imagine how vivid the tales Twain told his children were, but this is the only one he recorded a portion of. Philip and Erin Stead, my favorite author-illustrator team who also happen to be husband and wife, decided to "collaborate" with Twain and finish his story.

The Steads made a few changes to his narrative, such as swapping out some of the animals he mentioned for ones of their own choosing. And they filled in the gaps in the story, most notably by adding an ending, which Twain either never created or just didn't record in his notes.

The format of the book makes this collaboration evident. Philip narrates the story, occasionally pausing that narration to refer to Twain's recounting of the story to him. He even honors the fact that Twain did not finish the story with a note before the final section that tells how Twain got up to get some tea and never came back, leaving Philip to finish with his own imaginings.

This book made me think about what we could do with this model of finishing an author's story. What if, to help our children both engage with great literature and authors and delve into and enjoy their own writing, we took a cue from the Steads?

Here are some project ideas that could be completed individually or as part of an in-depth unit collaborating with great authors and writing between the lines.

1. Read to your children the first section of a classic story that they have not heard before, and then ask them to finish telling the story themselves. Talk about what they learned in the beginning about the setting, characters, and plot, and then encourage them to further develop these.

2. Illustrations can be used at each point in the process. After reading the initial section, have your children sketch what they have heard. As they plan out their story arc

to complete the narrative, encourage them to doodle along the way. And once the narrative is finished, they can illustrate the finished story. This can work for many ages and skill levels, starting with a picture book and going all the way up to a short novel.

3. Read a book in its entirety with your children, but pause at the end of each chapter or at important events in the plot. Either role-play a conversation with the author or have your children imagine and write down what they would ask the author if they were telling your children the story in person.

4. Pick an author that your children like and respect. Read a biography or other information about the author. Learn about their strengths and weaknesses, and have your children decide what positive aspect of this author they would like to help the world understand. Then either write a story under the author's "name" that highlights this aspect or take a story the author has already written and make some changes to bring out this quality even more.

5. Read all but the last chapter of a book. Brainstorm with your children what you think the author wrote for the ending. Also brainstorm how you would end the story if you were the author. Illustrate either of these endings for fun if you want. Then read the real ending of the book. If your guess about the ending was correct, talk about what foreshadowing, knowledge of the author, etc., led you to that idea. If your guess was way off, talk about why you think it was hard to understand where the author was going with the narrative. Discuss the similarities and differences between the ending you came up with and the author's ending.

Books are not a one-way street. They are conversations, and the more our children understand that, the more freedom they will be given to fall in love with the written word and with classics of literature, whether *Corduroy* or *Moby Dick*. The more they identify with authors and learn that they too can function as authors, the more confidence they will gain in all of their writing endeavors.

PETER PAN
BY J. M. BARRIE

For more than one hundred years, people all over the world have been swept away to Neverland while reading J. M. Barrie's *Peter Pan*. If your only exposure to this classic has been through the lens of Disney, you are in for quite an adventure. In the pages of this book, you'll find cultural divides, undesirable behaviors, and bits of darkness sprinkled throughout.

The book has some wildly imaginative themes. There are fun, vibrant characters and multiple adventures to act out. We are invited to play. We are invited to dream. We are invited to fly! And we do. *Peter Pan* is sad and joyous, funny and frightening. It touches deep within our childhood hearts and brings us back to our own Neverlands.

THE GATHERING

Any location where imaginations can soar is a good place for this book club. The ideal location would be a place where either the sea rolls or trees abound. You could even squeeze the festivities into a bedroom. But be sure to leave the window open!

We chose a location that brought us to "Mermaids' Lagoon," complete with a "Marooners' Rock" for Wendy to fly off on a kite! There were plenty of "Never Birds" for us to play with and trees to climb.

When you are out in nature, there is little need for decorations. But a few thoughtful elements from the story can add a touch of whimsy to the gathering. A color palette of green, gold, and brown with these items will look lovely:

- A star made out of tree branches
- A golden crocodile

- A vintage clock

- A gold vintage lantern

- Old wooden crates

- A native drum

- A homemade kite made out of green fabric

- Peter's flute

- A toy bow and arrow set

Having these items available allowed all sorts of beautiful, imaginative play to occur organically for the children.

FOOD IDEAS

Here are some foods, based on the book, that you could serve:

- Nuts: "He had brought nuts for the boys."

- Hook's catch of the day (Goldfish crackers)

- Green grapes and green apples

- Green sugar cake: "Cook a large rich cake of a jolly thickness with green sugar on it."

- Hot tea with milk and sugar: "Would you like an adventure now? Or would you like to have your tea first?"
- Pixie punch (green juice; see the recipe)
- Peter's medicine (water)

HOW TO MAKE PIXIE PUNCH

1. Dissolve two boxes of lime Jell-O and 1 cup sugar in 1 cup boiling water.

2. Pour the mixture into a punch bowl, and add 1 can (46 ounces) pineapple juice, 2 cans frozen orange juice concentrate, and 1 quart cold water. Mix together.

3. Before serving, add 2 liters ginger ale and ice.

DISCUSSION QUESTIONS

1. What does Peter lose in the Darlings' nursery?

2. When are fairies born?

3. What does Wendy give to Peter as a kiss? What does Peter give to Wendy?

4. What happens to Wendy as she is flying into Neverland for the first time?

5. What is Captain Hook most afraid of? Why does the crocodile make a "tick tick tick" sound?

6. When do mermaids come up in extraordinary numbers? And what do they do?

7. How does Wendy avoid drowning on her first encounter with Hook?

8. How does Peter avoid drowning after his first conflict with Hook since returning to Neverland?

9. What does Peter put the bird eggs in before boarding the Never Bird nest?

10. What do the Redskins do when they have a victory? (Based on your group, this could be a good place to talk about how language changes over time in how we refer to people and groups of people.)

11. Who saves Peter from drinking the medicine that Hook poisoned?

12. What does Peter do to save Tink's life?

13. Who is your favorite character in the book? Why?

14. Discuss the character of Peter Pan. What do you like about him? What are his weaknesses?

15. Would you want a dog for a nanny? Why?

16. Why do wonderful thoughts lift you up? What are the opposite of lovely, wonderful thoughts? What do you think those thoughts do?

ACTIVITIES

MAKE EDIBLE TEEPEES

MATERIALS

Kitchen scissors

Sugar cones (one for each child)

Popsicle sticks

Tub of frosting

Pretzel sticks

Piping frosting (optional)

INSTRUCTIONS

1. Using kitchen scissors, cut the point off of each ice cream cone, about ½ inch, so that there is enough room for one or two pretzel sticks to fit through.

2. With a popsicle stick, spread the frosting in the small opening of the cone.

3. Break a few pretzel sticks into different sizes, dip the ends into frosting, and place them into the point of the cone. Hold them in place for a few seconds so that they stick.

4. Use the piping frosting to decorate the teepee, if desired.

5. Freeze for 15 minutes so that the frosting hardens.

 **SAFETY TIP**

Using scissors can be dangerous and should be done with adult supervision.

DRAW A MAP OF NEVERLAND

MATERIALS

A copy of *Peter Pan*

Cardstock

Colored pencils and crayons

INSTRUCTIONS

Review the book's descriptions of Neverland, then draw the different parts of Neverland on the cardstock, coloring and labeling the map as you go.

PARTY FAVORS

- "Mermaid" bubbles
- Pixie dust and bells
- Crocodile gummies
- Thimble and acorn "kisses"

BY JENNIFER NARAKI

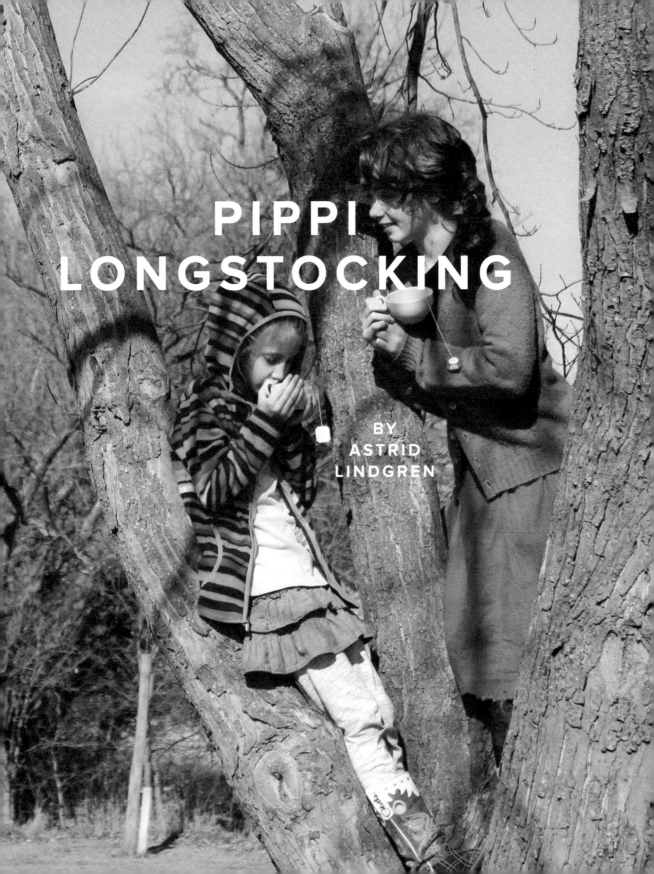

PIPPI LONGSTOCKING

BY
ASTRID
LINDGREN

As a young girl, I laughed my way through this classic by Astrid Lindgren, taking delight in Pippi's outrageous endeavors and the ridiculous stories she invents. As an adult reading to my children, I found her just as amusing and endearing but with some added layers of depth I hadn't noticed before.

At first glance, Pippi seems lacking in manners, making her perhaps less than ideal as a role model. But if you look past some of the antics, the exaggeration, and the sometimes seemingly careless behavior, you'll see a girl who is inventive, generous, friendly, heroic, quick to apologize, and eager to please.

She knows she won't always get it right, and like all of us, she hopes to be loved, invited, and accepted anyway. She is confident, resilient, and courageous, and those are pretty strong redeeming qualities, even stronger than Pippi's remarkable muscles, and certainly traits I hope for in my children and myself.

THE GATHERING

The book lends itself to a variety of vistas, even if you don't happen to live in an old majestic house like Villa Villekulla with a tumbledown garden gate, a gravel path bordered with old moss-covered trees (really good climbing trees), and a horse on the porch. Here are some ideas for the book club:

- A picnic in a pasture, a park, or your backyard
- A coffee party like Tommy and Annika's in your own house
- A celebration like Pippi's birthday party in your kitchen, parlor, or attic

"My name is Pippilotta Delicatessa Windowshade Mackrelmint Efraim's Daughter Longstocking!"

—Astrid Lindgren, *Pippi Longstocking*

For decoration for your *Pippi Longstocking* event, consider the following ideas:

- An old suitcase overflowing with treasure and gold coins
- A collection of natural curiosities, shells, and/or trinkets from other countries
- A little stuffed monkey like Mr. Nilsson
- A toy horse
- A painting or drawing of an old house like Villa Villekulla
- Tea and coffee items
- Small items related to the circus, policemen, the fire department, or ships

FOOD IDEAS

The picnic Pippi packs for Tommy and Annika provides delicious inspiration for the menu, as does the infamous coffee party and Pippi's birthday party. This book is not lacking in food references!

- Ham and cheese sandwiches
- Swedish meatballs

- Miniature smoked sausages
- Carrots and apples (for the horse)
- Bananas (for Mr. Nilsson)
- Pineapple pudding (vanilla pudding in small dishes topped with a pineapple ring and a cherry)
- Pancakes
- Tea cakes
- A cream pie with a red candy on top
- Coffee with cream and sugar
- Hot chocolate with whipped cream
- Heart-shaped *pepparkakor* (Swedish ginger cookies; recipes available online)

DISCUSSION QUESTIONS

1. Do you remember Pippi's full name?

2. What happened to Pippi's parents?

3. What are the advantages and disadvantages of living alone as a child without any adults?

4. What do you think attracts Pippi, Tommy, and Annika to each other, and what strengthens their friendship?

5. Why do you think Pippi makes up stories about her world travels and experiences?

6. How does Pippi handle a bully? Is this how you would deal with someone who is unkind? Why or why not?

7. What did Pippi do that made you laugh the most?

8. What is something silly Pippi does in the book that you have done yourself? What thing do you wish you could try?

9. Pippi is a "thing-finder." What is the most exciting thing you have ever found on the ground, and what did you do with it?

ACTIVITIES

THING-FINDER SCAVENGER HUNT

MATERIALS

Paper

Pen or pencil

Trinkets for hidden treasure

INSTRUCTIONS

Create a list of things to find that are appropriate for the setting of your gathering. Divide the participants into teams, and have them go searching for the items on the list. After each team completes the list, give them a clue to find the hidden treasure you have planted for them in a fun spot. You can hide multiple treasures for each of the teams to find.

SCRUBBING VACATION RELAY

This relay race is inspired by Pippi's hilarious stunt of scrubbing the floor with brushes attached to her feet!

MATERIALS

Whistle

4 scrub brushes with flat backs

4 lengths of string, 12 to 24 inches each

INSTRUCTIONS

Divide the participants into two teams and have half of each team gather at opposite ends of the floor you intend to "scrub." At the whistle, one member of each team ties a brush to each foot and "scrubs" their way across the floor as quickly as possible without losing the brushes. At the other end, they switch with someone on their team, and that person makes the return pass across the floor with the brushes and switches with someone waiting on that end. The first team to send every member across the room wins.

PARTY FAVORS

- Tin cans filled with cookies
- Little wooden toy daggers with jewels glued to the handles
- Tiny kraft paper boxes with a shell glued to the top
- Small bags of caramel candies
- Leather-bound notepads and silver pencils
- Toy flutes
- Butterfly pins
- Chocolate gold coins

BY RAIMIE HARRISON

ROBIN HOOD

BY HOWARD PYLE

Robin Hood (the full title is *The Merry Adventures of Robin Hood*) was selected for our book club by a family with a little boy who wanted a book with lots of fun and adventure. He also wanted things like sword fights and costumes. We wondered whether, with the complicated language, our kids would enjoy the book. Could they follow along?

It turns out they could. Our kids not only followed along with the book, but they actually fell in love with it. The language took a bit of time to get used to, and our family chose to listen to an audiobook because the narrator was a much better reader than I was. After a very short time, it really wasn't much of a struggle for the kids to understand what was going on in the book. And for the times it was confusing, reading it together allowed us to explain things to one another. In the end, *Robin Hood* made for a fun book club gathering!

THE GATHERING

A wooded area reminiscent of Sherwood Forest is the ideal location. Any park or yard with some trees and an open grassy area perfect for sword and cudgel fighting will work well. Kids can come in costumes as queens, ladies-in-waiting, friars, Merry Men, and Robin Hood too.

FOOD IDEAS

You can make your Robin Hood feast as extravagant or as simple as you want. Some food suggestions follow, and remember that, whether you're doing a full meal or an afternoon tea, spreading the food duties among the guests makes the gathering more manageable and fun!

- Meat pasties
- Cold chicken
- Roasted potatoes
- Pickles
- Oaten cakes
- Bread
- Butter
- English sticky toffee pudding with custard sauce
- Bottles of root beer and ginger ale for quaffing

DISCUSSION QUESTIONS

1. Who is your favorite character in *Robin Hood*? Can you explain why?

2. What is your favorite part of the book? What do you like about it?

3. Who is your least favorite character in the book? Why?

4. Do you know why they drank so much mead and ale instead of water in the days of *Robin Hood*?

5. What parts of the book are funny?

6. What is an outlaw? Is an outlaw always a bad person? Can an outlaw be a good person? Can you think of an example?

7. Why does Robin Hood first become an outlaw?

8. After Robin Hood begins living in Sherwood Forest, what does he see is happening to the peasants there? What does he decide to do about it?

9. Do you think Robin Hood is a good guy or a bad guy? Why?

10. Do you think there are some lessons you can learn from the book? Can you share an example of one of those lessons?

ACTIVITIES

Let the kids bring foam swords, run around, and get lost in their own magical, make-believe world. *Robin Hood* really lends itself to that kind of play. You can set up a few archery stations where kids can play with toy bows and arrows, or organize jousting tournaments and pretend sword and cudgel fights. Play games of tag, capture the flag, and statues.

PARTY FAVORS

- Play swords or toy bows and arrows
- Small bags of toy treasures

BY GRETA ESKRIDGE

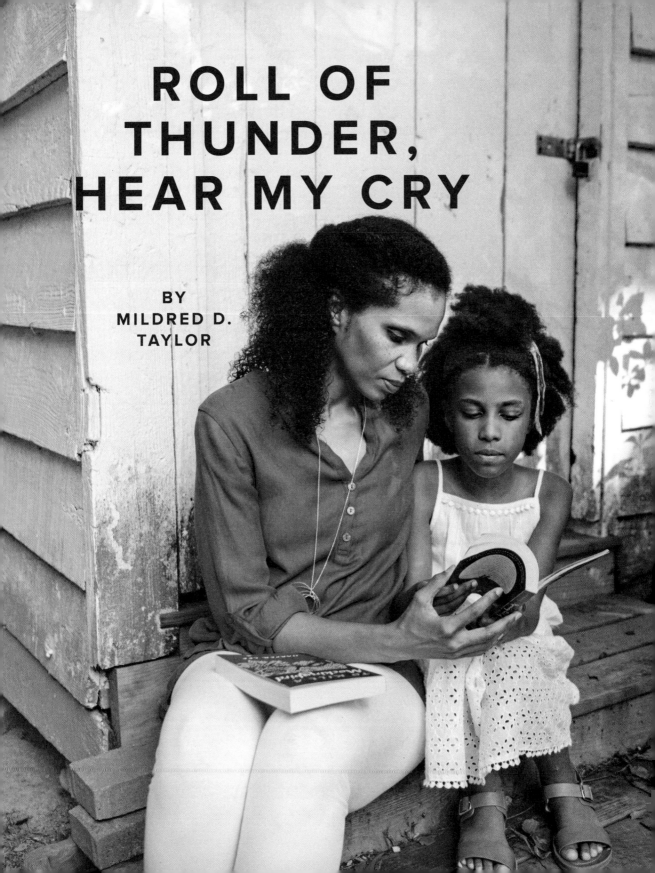

ROLL OF THUNDER, HEAR MY CRY

BY MILDRED D. TAYLOR

I was first introduced to *Roll of Thunder, Hear My Cry* in fourth grade, and this historical novel, told in the voice of nine-year-old Cassie Logan, single-handedly changed my relationship with literature. The beautifully raw tale touched me in ways no other story ever had. It brought my history lessons to life while helping me understand the realities of injustice and the power of storytelling.

The book, which follows a Black family's life in rural Mississippi during the Great Depression, does not shy away from the hard realities of racism, segregation, Jim Crow, and even lynching. The story line is honest and does not hold back, but nothing is shared for shock value; it is all necessary to the plot. The book also delves deeply into themes of family, community, friendship, and education. One of my children cried when the book was over because she was not ready for the story to end—a true testament to the emotional power of this installment of the Logan family saga.

THE GATHERING

Land is a major theme of the book; it symbolizes the Logan family's deeply rooted generational bonds, provides respite during tumultuous times, and represents independence from oppressive sharecropping. A perfect setting for this gathering is a simple outdoor space like a backyard, a park or preserve, a wooded or lakeside setting, or a nature center.

FOOD IDEAS

Everyday meals and special foods are subtly woven throughout the story to help characterize times of want and days of plenty.

To really connect with the Logans and their Mississippi roots, you can serve Southern foods like fried chicken, macaroni and cheese, collard greens, and candied yams, or you can focus on some of the other foods mentioned in the book:

- **CROWDER PEAS AND CORNBREAD**: These beans were brought to America from Africa back in the 1600s, and like black-eyed peas, crowder peas are ideal for soul food dishes.

- **BISCUITS**: Hot bread is a daily staple the Logan family has to cut back on when their flour, sugar, and baking

powder begin running low. Biscuits can be served on their own or alongside ham or bacon.

- **SWEET POTATO PIE, EGG CUSTARD PIE, OR RICH BUTTER POUND CAKE:** These desserts are prepared as part of the family's Christmas feast.

- **ROASTED PEANUTS:** If there are no nut allergies in your group, small paper bags of roasted peanuts can be handed out to snack on during the gathering.

DISCUSSION QUESTIONS

1. The title of the book is based on the epigraph (quote) at the beginning of chapter 11, which comes from an old "spiritual," poem, or chant. Why do you think the author chose to use those words as the title of the book?

2. Why is Miss Crocker satisfied with the old hand-me-down schoolbooks, and what does she mean when she says Mama is "biting the hand that feeds" her?

3. What leads to the boycott of the Wallace store, and why is it such a big deal?

How does it impact the Black community? The white community?

4. How do you feel about the way Lillian Jean and her family treat Cassie on the street in Strawberry? What do you think about how Cassie gets back at her?

5. Why is Stacey and T.J.'s relationship so complicated? Why is Stacey willing to risk so much to help T.J. after the robbery? Have you ever navigated a complicated friendship?

6. Family is a major theme of the book. Give some examples that demonstrate the importance of family to the Logans and their friends.

7. How did the Logans come to have the land they live on, and why is it so important that they keep it? What are some of the sacrifices they make to keep their land?

8. Have you ever had to make a sacrifice to protect something or someone you care about? Tell us about it.

9. How do you feel about where you live? How important is it to you?

10. Which character can you relate to most, and why?

11. If you could interview one character, who would it be, and what would you ask?

12. What are the differences between Jefferson Davis County School and Great Faith Elementary and Secondary School? Think about transportation, books and resources, annual schedule, location, and more.

13. The US Flag Code states, "No other flag or pennant should be placed above or, if on the same level, to the right of the flag of the United States of America." Jefferson Davis County School flies the Mississippi flag higher than the American flag. What is the significance of the transposed flags?

14. In chapter 8, T.J. says that he has too many problems of his own to worry about "Cassie Uncle Tomming Lillian Jean." This is a reference to Harriet Beecher Stowe's novel *Uncle Tom's Cabin*, but what does the term "Uncle Tomming" mean? Do you agree with T.J.'s assessment of Cassie's behavior?

15. In the middle of chapter 9, Papa compares the family's relationship to the land to a fig tree. Explain the meaning behind his metaphor.

16. Who started the fire in the cotton field, and why? What do you think about the fire? What would you have done?

17. In the last line of the book, Cassie says, "I cried for T.J. For T.J and the land." What does she mean?

18. This book won the Newbery Medal in 1977 as the most distinguished American children's book published the previous year. What do you think it was about this book that led the committee to choose it over all the other books that year?

ACTIVITIES

COMMUNITY FOOD BASKETS

Create baskets of much-needed food staples to be donated to neighbors or community organizations in need, just as the Logans provide food for others within their close-knit community.

MATERIALS

Tissue paper

Baskets or cardboard boxes covered in
pretty paper

Canned goods and packaged foods

PROTEINS: canned chicken, canned tuna,
dry beans, peanut butter

GRAINS: rice, pasta, oatmeal, grits,
granola bars, boxed meals

FRUITS AND VEGGIES: canned tomatoes
and green beans, dried fruit, applesauce,
fruit cups

STAPLES: cooking oils, spices/seasonings,
flour, sugar

Glue Dots or double-sided tape

Cellophane wrap or cellophane bags

Roll of wide, wired ribbon

Scissors

Single-sided clear tape

INSTRUCTIONS

1. Add a layer of tissue paper to the bottom of your basket to help support the contents.

2. Set one of your sturdiest food items in the center, with taller items around and behind it. Place smaller items in front and use tissue paper to fill gaps. Use Glue Dots to attach items together and prevent sliding.

3. Place the entire basket on top of several cellophane sheets. Gather the cellophane at the top, twist the ends, and tie a ribbon around it. Fold and tape down any remaining cellophane flaps.

 SAFETY TIP

Using scissors can be dangerous and should be done with adult supervision.

SWEET POTATO
PIE IN A JAR

Mini sweet potato pies made in individual widemouthed mason jars will invoke the festive Logan homemaking spirit.

MATERIALS

Half-pint widemouthed mason jars (one for each guest)

Refrigerated pie crusts

Sweet potato pie filling

INSTRUCTIONS

1. Preheat the oven to 350°F.

2. Cut the pie crusts into circles that will fit inside the jars. Press the crust into the bottom of the jar and up the sides.

3. Follow your favorite recipe for sweet potato pie and pour the mixture into the jars.

4. Bake for 40 minutes, or until a knife inserted in the center comes out clean.

5. Set aside on the counter to cool completely. Serve immediately with fresh whipped cream or refrigerate for later.

🧰 SAFETY TIP

Please exercise caution when baking with untempered glass jars. You could also make these in a muffin tin and transfer to a glass jar after they're baked. Use adult supervision with the oven and when cutting pie crusts.

WREATH ORNAMENTS

Make these small wreath ornaments to decorate a Christmas tree or another festive area of the home.

MATERIALS

Green beads
Red beads
Red pipe cleaners (one per wreath)
Scissors
Green ribbon

INSTRUCTIONS

1. String four green beads and one red bead onto a pipe cleaner. Repeat this pattern until you fill the length of the pipe cleaner.

INSTRUCTIONS

Read a few fables aloud and discuss their meanings. Work together in small groups to come up with original animal-based fables with lessons or morals found in *Aesop's Fables*. Come back together and take turns sharing the fables. See if others can guess each group's intended lesson.

2. Push the beads into the center, leaving the pipe cleaner exposed on both ends. Bend the pipe cleaner into a circle, and twist the ends to make a small bow.

3. Cut a green ribbon to 12 inches and attach it to the center for hanging your wreath.

CREATE YOUR OWN FABLE

Cassie's mother is an educator, and the Logans appreciate good literature. Use this inspiration to create fables to share with the group.

PARTY FAVORS

- **BAGS OF LEMON DROPS:** Mr. Jamison, a lawyer who is always kind to the Logans, stops by the house one afternoon with a fruit cake and a bag of lemon drops for each child.

- **STOCKINGS OR BURLAP BAGS FILLED WITH LICORICE, ORANGES, AND BANANAS:** The "once-a-year" store-bought candy and fruit help fill the Logan children's stockings on Christmas morning.

BY AMBER O'NEAL JOHNSTON

MATERIALS

A copy of *Aesop's Fables*
Paper and pens (optional)

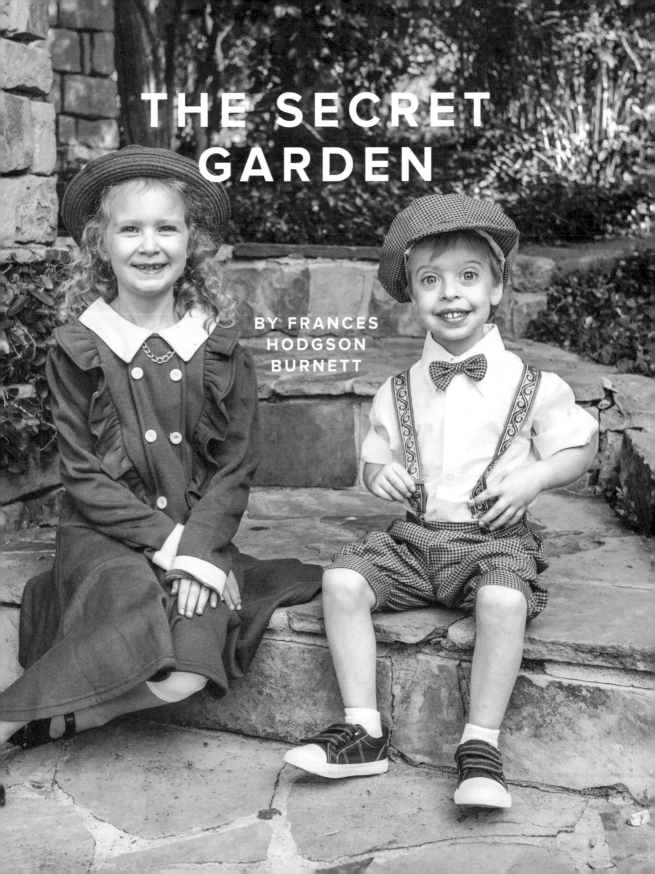

THE SECRET GARDEN

BY FRANCES HODGSON BURNETT

The Secret Garden by Frances Hodgson Burnett was my favorite book as a child, and I was excited to share it with my children. It's also a perfect pick for book clubs. Woven in its pages are themes of adventure, wonder, and self-discovery. The characters are easy to invest in, and each chapter provoked great conversations with my child while we read together. Note that the early pages may require extra navigation for sensitive hearts.

THE GATHERING

A park, botanical garden, backyard, or community garden would all be great options for your gathering. If you're meeting in a public place, try for early morning so it won't be as crowded and there will be space for the children to run around.

Gather some story-related props to inspire their play, including jump ropes, keys, and plush toys of animals in the book. It wasn't long before my son grabbed a stuffed fox and declared he was Dickon; another child began counting his jumps with the rope as Mary did.

FOOD IDEAS

Plan a picnic and keep the food light and easy. *The Secret Garden* lists a variety of foods that are easy to prepare and share with the group. The items below are mentioned in the book and provide ample inspiration for an event:

- **FRUITS AND VEGETABLES**

  Blackberries
  Carrots
  Turnips
  Cabbage
  Radish
  Onion

- **BAKED GOODS**

  Cake
  Bread and butter
  Buns with currants
  Biscuits
  Toast
  Dough-cake
  Hot oak cake
  Muffins
  Roasted potato crumpets
  Crusty cottage loaf

- **BEVERAGES**

  Hot tea
  Milk with cream
  Buttermilk

- **MEAT**

  Bacon
  Ham
  Chicken
  Beef

- **SWEET TREATS**

  Pudding
  Marmalade
  Raspberry jam
  Honey
  Treacle (molasses)
  Clotted cream

- **BREAKFAST ITEMS**

  Eggs
  Porridge

DISCUSSION QUESTIONS

1. Did you like the book? Why or why not?

2. Who is your favorite character, and why? Least favorite?

3. What is the best part of the book?

4. Which character changes the most?

5. How does Mary learn to love others?

6. What is your favorite thing about being in nature?

7. How would you describe "the Magic" to someone who hasn't read the book?

8. How do Mary or Colin think about themselves at the end of the book compared with at the beginning of the book?

9. Many animals are mentioned in the book. Is there one that stands out to you?

10. What do you think will happen to the characters in the future?

11. Why was the garden locked up and kept a secret?

12. How are Mary and Dickon alike?

13. What makes Mary go searching the forbidden hallways?

14. Why does Mary treat everyone so rudely?

15. Why does Dickon get along so well with animals?

16. How does Mary change throughout the story? Does she change physically or mentally or both?

17. What does it mean that Mary is "disagreeable" looking? How does this reflect her inner state of being?

18. Why do the nurse and doctor suspect that Colin may not be sick anymore?

19. What do Mary and Colin do to throw off their suspicion?

20. How is Dickon's upbringing different from Mary's and Colin's?

21. What is it that brings Archibald Craven (Colin's father) back home?

22. Colin says, "I am sure there is Magic in everything, only we have not sense enough to get hold of it and make it do things for us." What is the magic that Colin talks about in this book?

TERRARIUM

MATERIALS

Glass containers (each child can bring their own)

2 cups small pebbles

¾ cup activated charcoal

¾ cup sphagnum moss

2 to 3 cups soil

1 or 2 small plants per child

Ziplock bags

1 small metal key per child

INSTRUCTIONS

Ahead of time, measure the materials into small bags for easy distribution and assembly. On the day of your gathering, give the children the bags that hold the pebbles, activated charcoal, sphagnum moss, soil, and plants, and instruct them to put the ingredients in their jar in that order, patting down each layer. When they've finished, give each child a small metal key that they can drop in the terrarium or bury in their very own secret garden.

TREASURE HUNT

MATERIALS

Key

Sidewalk chalk

INSTRUCTIONS

Before everyone arrives, hide a special key somewhere in the area—in a garden, behind bushes, or by a tree. (I found skeleton keys at a craft store in the $1 section.) Don't bury it too deep. Create a clue. I drew a door with chalk on our backyard fence and buried the key very close by. I piled a few leaves and rocks on the spot as well. I told the children their clue was "secret door." The finder gets to keep the special key. Let the finder of the buried key bask in their victory for a few minutes, but then surprise the other kids with their own special keys.

START A GARDEN

MATERIALS

Tiny paper cups

Soil

A few different packets of seeds

INSTRUCTIONS

Arrange the materials on a table in the order listed above. When the kids arrive, show them how to put the soil in a cup and plant some seeds to take home and grow. Talk to them about giving their plants the proper sunlight and water and encourage them to take responsibility for their garden.

PARTY FAVORS

The kids will take home their terrarium, special key, and planted seeds. Another idea is to paint some wooden elephants white so each child can have their own "ivory" elephant.

BY MANDY LACKEY

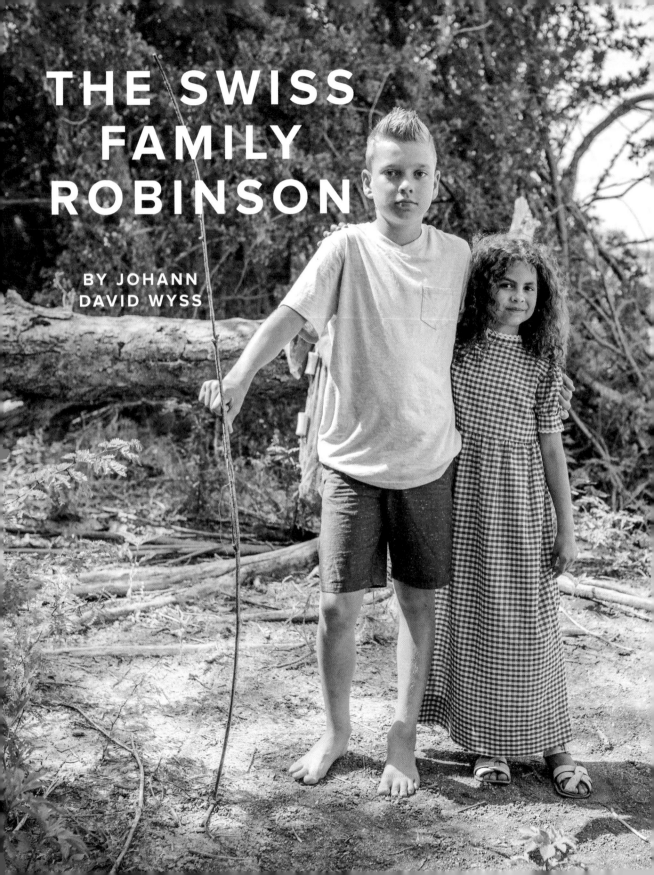

THE SWISS FAMILY ROBINSON

BY JOHANN DAVID WYSS

When I was a little girl, I imagined that I was a castaway on a deserted island. I practiced survival skills and made friends with sea creatures, such as turtles and dolphins. I don't believe I'm the only child who has done this. There's just something about an island adventure that gets the imagination running wild. When I read *The Swiss Family Robinson* with my family, we enjoyed exploring the story and imagining how we would live on our own tropical island.

THE GATHERING

The book's island vibe can be easily captured at home with bunches of tropical flowers, palm fronds, and island music streaming on Pandora. You can keep it simple, but even a few special touches will make the environment extra special for the children.

FOOD IDEAS

For refreshments, consider these ideas:

- Tropical fruit skewers
- Hawaiian pizzas
- Fruity drinks with paper umbrellas in them

If possible, have some real sugar cane for the kids to try, just like the Robinsons find on their island. If you make "regular" food items, give them creative names, such as "Ostrich Egg Salad" and "Baarrrrbecue Chips."

As a fun activity, get some fresh coconuts and have the adults crack them open. Give each child a taste of the water and meat inside. Many kids have never tasted fresh coconut, and it is a neat experience for them.

DISCUSSION QUESTIONS

1. Who are the main characters?

2. How do the Robinsons end up on the island?

3. How does the family get to shore?

4. What kinds of animals are on the ship?

5. What items from the ship do they decide to take to shore with them?

6. What is the first thing they find on the island?

7. What does Elizabeth bring from the ship that turns out to be very useful?

8. What attacks Jack in the water?

9. What useful substance does Ernest discover?

10. How do they fool the monkeys into helping them?

11. What does the dog Turk kill? What does Fritz get as a result of Turk's kill?

12. What do they eat for dinner when they get back to the beach?

13. What do they decide to do the next morning? What items do they bring back?

14. Where do they build their first home? What does Father have to build first?

15. Describe the tree house. What do they name it?

16. The boys go back to the shipwreck for supplies. What does Father do on their last trip?

17. How does Ernest train the eagle? What does the eagle respond to after it is trained?

18. What do the family members do when stuck in the tree house?

19. What kills Grizzle?

20. What does Fritz find on the other side of the island?

21. What visitors come to the island?

22. Who decides to go back to Europe?

MESSAGE IN A BOTTLE

The Robinsons are happy on their island and never try to make contact with the rest of the world. However, this fun activity gets kids thinking about what kind of message they would send if they were shipwrecked on a tropical island.

MATERIALS

Paper

Pens

Glass bottles

Corks

INSTRUCTIONS

1. Give the children a sheet of paper and have them write a message or draw a picture.

2. When they are finished, help them roll up their paper into a scroll and insert it into a bottle.

3. Have them put a cork in the top and encourage the parents to help their children send their messages by tossing them into a swimming pool, a creek, or a pond where they can be retrieved after they're finished.

WOODBURNING

I'm pretty sure there were no wood burners on the tropical island the Robinsons found themselves living on. But I do know kids love to use a wood burner. It's a fun and easy-to-learn handicraft.

⊞ SAFETY TIP

Parental supervision is advised for children of all ages, but especially for the younger ones, when using wood burners.

MATERIALS

Wood burner (available at craft stores and online)

Small round tree slices (available at craft stores and online, or make your own!)

INSTRUCTIONS

Depending on how many wood burners you have, you may need to have the kids rotate through the various activity stations. Give each child a small tree round. Explain that the wood burner is very hot and can burn them easily if they touch the tip. Show them how to hold it and make letters and symbols in the wood. Let them give it a try. They will quickly get the hang of it and beg to do more.

ISLAND JEWELRY

This activity was inspired by Fritz's discovery of a secret bay full of oysters with pearls.

MATERIALS

Jewelry cord

Faux pearl beads

Shells with holes drilled in them

INSTRUCTIONS

This is a fairly easy project. The littlest ones might need some help stringing the jewelry cord through the holes in the pearls or shells, but otherwise, just let them have fun creating. When they are finished, help them tie the ends together so they can wear their creation as a bracelet or a necklace.

PARTY FAVORS

The kids will get to take home their bottle, woodburning project, and island jewelry. But it's always fun to surprise them with a parting gift. Here are a few suggestions:

- Small bundles of tropical jellybeans tied up in cheesecloth and string

- Bags of seashells collected from the shore

- Homemade dehydrated tropical fruit, like pineapple or bananas

BY AINSLEY ARMENT

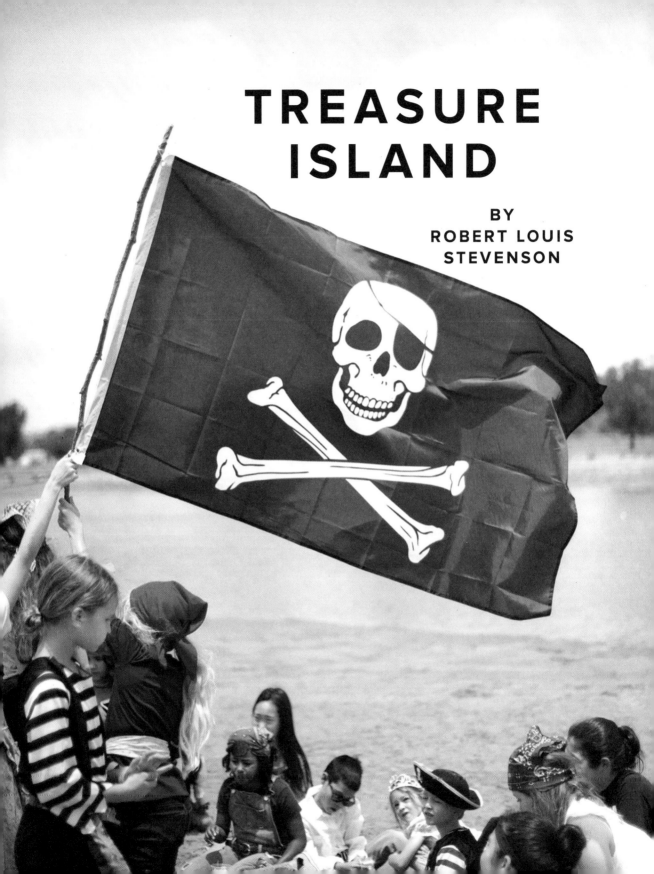

TREASURE ISLAND

BY
ROBERT LOUIS
STEVENSON

Published in 1883, Robert Louis Stevenson's *Treasure Island* is one of the most highly read adventure novels of all time. The story provokes consideration of moral dilemmas and challenges us to explore good and evil as buccaneers take us on an unforgettable journey to find buried treasure.

THE GATHERING

We are fortunate to live near the sea, so it was an easy decision for our book club to meet by the seaside. If you do not live near a body of water, a charming inn reminiscent of the Admiral Benbow could be a fun place to gather. A log house is also an important setting in the book, so that is another option.

FOOD IDEAS

We really enjoy making the book come to life by serving up a feast of foods mentioned within the pages. These are the items we enjoyed for *Treasure Island*:

- Kids' rum (apple cider)
- Kids' wine (grape juice)
- A meat and cheese tray
- Pickles and apples
- Goldfish crackers
- Pirate cake pops

DISCUSSION QUESTIONS

1. How does Jim Hawkins feel about the many different characters he meets in this book? Have you ever met an unusual character? Describe your feelings toward that person.

the flag of truce. Does Long John Silver have any positive traits?

5. What happened at the conference of the pirates after the unsuccessful attack on the log house?

6. Describe Dr. Livesey's conference with Long John Silver, where the bargain was made to surrender the chart and the stockade to the pirates.

7. Have you ever gone on a trip of exploration? Tell us about it.

8. What is a Jolly Roger, and what is its significance in the story?

9. Who are your favorite and least favorite characters, and why?

10. Discuss your favorite part of the story. What do you like about it?

11. Jim Hawkins says he's glad Long John Silver got away. What do you think of Jim's moral reasoning here? Are you glad that Long John Silver got away? Why or why not?

12. If you found a treasure map, would you risk your life to find the treasure? Was the treasure worth the death, pain, and sorrow it took to find it? Why or why not?

2. Tell a story in which some sound can be made highly significant, like the "tap-tap-tapping" of the blind man's stick in this book. For example: the sound of wind in the trees, the ticking of a clock, or the noise of the streets.

3. Describe Ben Gunn's attack on the pirate camp at night.

4. Give an account of Long John Silver's return to the pirates after his mission with

SHOOTING OFF CANNONS

Provide pop-its (small novelty fireworks safe for kids to throw onto the ground) and pull-string confetti bombs, and let the kids loose setting them off.

TREASURE HUNT

Before the gathering, hide a locked wooden box filled with trinkets and then the key in different locations. Have the children search for them. When they find the box and the key to open it, they can divvy up the treasure to take home.

COSTUMES AND FREE PLAY

We have found that when our children are wearing costumes, they naturally want to act out scenes from the book. We encourage that by offering plenty of free time to play and by strewing relevant items around the book club site. For this book, our props included a Jolly Roger flag; play swords, pistols, and cannon; a map and coins; a skeleton pointing the way to the treasure; and a handmade boat to represent the *Hispaniola*!

BY JENNIFER NARAKI

THE VANDERBEEKERS OF 141ST STREET

BY KARINA YAN GLASER

As mom to five kids, I am always on the lookout for stories about large families. So when we started *The Vanderbeekers of 141st Street*, we immediately embraced this large rambunctious family, whose house was always messy, whose kids were notorious for being terrible cooks but cooked nonetheless, and who were constantly crafting, reading, playing music, and conducting experiments.

These kids and their interests opened a whole world for us. Their passions became ours. We wanted to know what the songs sounded like that the eldest daughter was playing on her violin, if lemons really could power an LED, and what double-chocolate pecan cookies tasted like and why in the world we had never heard of them before.

The Vanderbeeker kids would never be found in front of a screen because they have too many other hobbies and interests to consume them. Discovering this counterculture family in a modern world lit our family with excitement, and we unknowingly set elements of this book into motion

in our own home, creating a family culture of exploration.

"The brownstone stood out not because of its architecture, but because of the constant hum of activity that burst out of it. Among the many people who had visited the Vanderbeeker household there was quite a bit of debate about what it was like, but general agreement about what it was
NOT:
Calm
Tidy
Boring
Predictable."

—Karina Yan Glaser,
The Vanderbeekers of 141st Street

THE GATHERING

Much of the story takes place in the Vanderbeekers' New York City brownstone, so make a cozy space in your own home, wherever it is. Read the story aloud together, and to enhance the reading experience, here's a music playlist with some songs based on characters and stories in the book:

- Vittorio Monti's "Csárdás"
- Beethoven concertos
- Dvořák's "Humoresque"
- Paganini's "Cantabile for Violin and Guitar"
- "La Folía"
- "Les Furies"
- "The Swan"

Mr. Beiderman is a jazz cat, so don't forget to include some Duke Ellington.

FOOD IDEAS

Food plays a big part in this book, as it should in a big family. This was one of our favorite elements of the book, as we got to try new recipes and added our favorites to our repertoire.

- Chocolate- or cheese-filled croissants
- Flourless chocolate cake
- Apple turnovers
- Jam cookies
- Cheesecake
- Carrot cake
- Soup with cheesy bread
- Beef stew with roasted veggies and a baguette

DISCUSSION QUESTIONS

1. The brownstone that the Vanderbeeker family lives in becomes almost a character in the story. Did you feel that if the Vanderbeekers had to move it would be like leaving a family member behind?

2. The author gives the brownstone feelings by describing it creaking and sighing through periods of sadness or hustle and bustle. This is called "anthropomorphism." Can you think of any other books that give human characteristics to animals or objects?

3. The timeline for the story is very rushed! Can you imagine having just under a week to move? What would you prioritize, and how would you pack?

4. The Vanderbeekers' neighbors are a huge part of their lives. What is your favorite story of the relationships formed within this Harlem neighborhood?

5. Could you draw the floor plan of your home without looking?

6. Why is it so important for Oliver to have a room of his own? How does he make the tiny space his own, and why does he want so badly to keep it?

7. The Vanderbeekers' pets are a huge part of the story, and they make it much more interesting. Which is your favorite?

8. What changes in Hyacinth when she becomes Hyacinth the Brave? Do you think giving yourself a superhero name could help you overcome a fear?

9. Why is Mr. Rochester so eager to sign the Vanderbeeker children's petition, even though he doesn't know them at all?

10. Do you think it's weird that the children have lived in their home so long and yet have never seen their landlord, who lives in the same building?

11. Each of the children brainstorms their own ideas for influencing the Beiderman to allow them to renew their lease. Which is your favorite idea? Does it work?

12. Each child thinks that something they like a lot (music for Isa, basketball for Oliver, for example) contributed to the Beiderman not liking them. Is this really the case?

13. When the Vanderbeeker children are finally invited into Mr. Beiderman's home, what do they find there?

14. Mr. Beiderman was changed by a horrific event. It's easy to see grumpy people and not think about what might have happened in their past. Did Mr. Beiderman's story change the way you feel about anyone in your life?

15. What was your reaction when Mr. Beiderman suddenly changed his mind? Are there foreshadowing statements within the book that softened this twist for you?

ACTIVITIES

SCIENCE EXPERIMENT

One of the girls in the book, Jessie, is a mad scientist. She builds a Rube Goldberg–type machine for watering the garden. If you have any science-minded kids, build something similar together. Don't be disappointed if your machine doesn't work. The value of this activity is in the process,

overcoming roadblocks and trying to figure out solutions when plans don't pan out. Alternatively, find a simple experiment to do with the kids that will get them excited about science!

COMMUNITY LETTER WRITING

Community is a major theme of this book. In the spirit of connecting with those we love, write letters to people you don't get to see as often as you'd like. Send cards to those who are sick or in need of some extra consideration.

HAIKU

Read a few haikus, discuss the format, and then practice writing your own!

BY ARISA CUEVAS

CONTRIBUTORS

AINSLEY ARMENT is the founder of Wild + Free, cofounder of Wild Explorers Club and the Wild + Free Farm Village, and host of the weekly *Wild + Free* podcast. She and her husband, Ben, are raising their five children (Wyatt, Dylan, Cody, Annie, and Millie) in Virginia Beach, Virginia. | @ainsl3y

ALI DOVER is the mother to three children and lives in Cambridgeshire, United Kingdom. Her biggest value is freedom. She loves photographing children. To Ali, their natural curiosity and expressions are a delight to capture. She dreams of taking her children on far-flung travels to meet in person some of the wonderful people she has met on Instagram. | @ali__dover

ALICIA BROWN and her husband, Jeremy, homeschool their four children in a beautiful mountain valley in northwestern Montana. Alicia loves making space for her children to be creative, explore, and grow naturally. Alicia shares inspirational iPhone photography tips for moms on her blog and has written a book called *Playful Pictures* to help moms capture joy-filled pictures of their own children. | @writeyouonmyheart

ALISON BLAKE is married to her high school sweetheart and is mama to three precious kiddos, whom she loves adventuring with in Southern California, where they live. She is a former homeschoolee turned enthusiastic homeschooler with a passion to use her gifts to bless others | @alijoyblake

AMBER O'NEAL JOHNSTON lives in Georgia nestled among pine trees, hammocks, and zip lines with her husband and their four children. When they have the chance, her family enjoys extended worldschooling trips to immerse themselves in other cultures. Amber blogs at Heritage Mom.com. | @heritagemomblog

ANA OHLANDT is thankful for the opportunities she's had in life as an immigrant, a military spouse, and a travel addict—opportunities that have shaped her into the photographer and human that she is today. Her kids will forever be her muse but also her guides to keep pushing her forward with new challenges. | @anaohlandtphotography

ARISA CUEVAS is an English literature major living in Southern California with her five kids, two dogs, seven loads of laundry, and one husband. Her favorite thing is adventuring with her kids, whether it be filling a day-pack with snacks and hitting the road in search of a trail, or cuddling on the couch and traveling through characters in their read-alouds.

BRIANNE BUSKEY met her sweet husband at a high school summer camp. She loves to cook, visit new places, and dabble in all things creative and homemade. She was a reluctant homeschooling mom who fell in love with it over the years through much refining of her own. She loves sarcasm, iced coffee, donuts, and lots of laughing. | @brebuskey

BRIT CHAMBERS and her family live in the mountains of Virginia at the Wild + Free Farm Village. They love exploring the land and charting all the new plants and animals they've encountered since moving from their tiny home in Texas. A mom through foster care and adoption, Brit is an avid advocate for orphan prevention and loves traveling the world to share the gift of clean water, along with her love for Jesus. | @chasing.pure.simplicity

DANA NOWELL is a wife and mother of four. As a home educator, she thrives off learning alongside her crew through good books, games, and exploring. When she's not taking care of her family, she loves to play board games, sew, and encourage others. | @ourhexagonalhome

ELSIE IUDICELLO lives in South Florida with her husband, four young boys, twenty-six chickens, two turkeys, a pig, and a pup. She is a writer, blogger, herder of small children, seeker of adventure, and avoider of laundry. She is passionate about encouraging homeschool moms, reading beautiful books, kissing her hubby, and raising her boys to be men of God. She loathes cat memes with poor spelling and the sound of squeaking Styrofoam. | farmhouseschoolhouse.com | @farmhouse_schoolhouse

GRETA ESKRIDGE is a joy-choosing, adventure-seeking, beauty-loving, homeschooling mama to three boys and one girl. She's married to an artist who fills their home and their lives with color and fun. It is her hope to be an encouragement to other mamas to live the most beautiful life they can, caring for themselves and their families, and finding joy and purpose in life along the way. | @maandpamodern

HANNAH MAYO is a writer and photographer with a heart for storytelling, adventure, and human connection. She lives in South Florida with her husband and three children and has been homeschooling since her eldest was in kindergarten. She is constantly seeking simplicity in her efforts to balance motherhood and marriage, business and home. She nurtures herself through books, journaling, watercolors, time in nature, yoga, and her sacred early morning quiet time. | @hmayophoto

JENNIFER DEES and her husband live in Long Beach, California. She homeschools her four children using the Charlotte Mason philosophy of education. She also makes oil paintings in her spare time. | @jendydees

JENNIFER PEPITO lives with her husband and seven children in California when they're not traveling the world. She has been homeschooling for twenty years and pulls much of her inspiration for learning with her children from Maria Montessori and Charlotte Mason. She is the founder of the Peaceful Press and author of *Bountiful Homeschooling on a Budget*. | @jenniferpepito

JENNIFER NARAKI was a beloved part of the Wild + Free community who passed away in 2019 after a long battle with cancer. She was a homeschooling mama of three boys, married for seventeen years to the man she met and fell for when she was seventeen. If you wanted to find her in a large, crowded room, you looked for the one with the loudest laugh. She delighted in grace, her boys, nature, books, music, vintage, fine fare, and photography. | @jennifernaraki

JILLIAN RAGSDALE, her husband, and two girls live an adventure-seeking and joy-filled life in the Dallas–Fort Worth area, where they try to spend as much time outdoors as possible. She wants to show her girls how to see and appreciate the beauty everywhere. | @ourgreennest

KAYLA SMITH stumbled upon her love for photography soon after purchasing her first DSLR camera with the desire to use it for video. She enjoys relationships with people and helping them capture those priceless moments that we can never get back. Kayla resides in Orlando, Florida.

KERI ANN SWAIM-GAMEZ is a California native who proudly lives in the Inland Empire. She is an energetic optimist who adores dogs, coffee, and snapping pictures. She is a full-time special education teacher, wife, daughter, auntie, friend, and fur-mom. She is madly in love with her scientist of a husband. | @keriannswaim

KIRSTY LARMOUR is part of a little international family: she, her husband, and her two daughters were each born in a different country. She is a lifestyle photographer who suffers from extreme wanderlust and is often found documenting how kids see the world. This usually involves taking lots of photos of her daughters' backs as they adventure through life. | kirstylarmour.com | @kirstylarmour

LESLIE MARTINO is a wife and home-schooling mom to four children who keep her on her toes. Over the last twenty years, Leslie has taught at both the elementary school and college level and in the dance/movement/fitness industry. She blogs at lesliemartino.com. | @lesliemmartino

MANDY LACKEY and her husband, Jeromy, live and play in northern Texas. They enjoy exploring the Dallas–Fort Worth area together and sharing experiences with their two children, Paisley and Fox. Mandy worked in the environmental science field and was inspired to begin homeschooling four years ago. She loves how home education exposes every member of the family to wonderful literature and discoveries. | mandybeth.com | @mandybethlackey

NICOLE ELIASON is a natural light photographer who lives in the suburbs of Atlanta and is doing her best to archive as many memories of her family as she can. She loves using her lens in new ways to capture moments for other families and athletes. | @nicoleeliasonphotography

NAOMI OVANDO lives with her husband and children in sunny Southern California. She's been homeschooling her two boys and little girl from the start. She can often be found going on adventures with her family in the nearby mountains or at the beach with camera in tow. | @3bebesmama

RAIMIE HARRISON nests happily amid her vintage trinkets on the Nebraska prairie with her hardworking husband. Their four children fill her days with noise, laughter, learning, messes, and the intense need for coffee. A deep love for literature, imaginative play, creativity, thankful memories of her own home education, and the search for a gentle and diligent way to nurture and teach her troop led Raimie to the Charlotte Mason method. | @joyfinderspath

RENEE HUSTON is a mother, teacher, and a chai latte drinker. She recently moved from the suburbs of DC to a nineteenth-century farmhouse with her husband and three kids. She loves being surrounded by nature and her neighbor's fifty-acre sheep farm. As a former public school teacher, Renee enjoys using her love for teaching to homeschool her own kids. In her free time, she enjoys hiding in her hammock swing to read, playing cards with her son, and writing new blog posts. | reneehuston.com | @rmhuston

SHARON MCKEEMAN is an author, educator, artist, and photographer. She is married and has three children whom she has homeschooled since the oldest was in kindergarten. She has experienced pregnancy loss and has three children in heaven. On her blog she writes honest encouragement for women walking through daily life and grief, and she is completing her memoir on pregnancy loss. She calls sunny Southern California home and loves spending time outdoors with her family. | @sharonmckeeman

STEPHANIE BEATY is a blessed mama of four children who lives in Florida, where she and her husband are renovating a small river cottage. After a ten-year career as a professional writer and public relations pro in New York City, London, Atlanta, and San Diego, she began Lifeography, a modern portrait business where she focuses on capturing relationships and connections for families and commercial opportunities. | @lifeographer

ABOUT
WILD + FREE

Wild + Free is a community of families who believe children not only should receive a quality education but also are meant to experience the adventure, freedom, and wonder of childhood. Wild + Free exists to equip families with resources to raise and educate children at home, as well as to encourage and inspire them along the way.

To learn more about Wild + Free and join the community,
visit bewildandfree.org. | @wildandfree.co

CREDITS

Photographs for the "Bringing Books to Life" essay on pages viii–xi by Kirsty Larmour. Used with permission. Photographs for the "How to Host a Book Club" essay on pages xii–3 by Alison Blake. Used with permission. Photographs of the *Adventures of Tom Sawyer* activity on pages 4–9 by Alicia Brown. Used with permission. Photographs of the *Anne of Green Gables* activity on pages 10–14 by Jennifer Naraki. Used with permission. Photographs of the *Around the World in Eighty Days* activity on pages 16–18 by Kirsty Larmour. Used with permission. Photographs of the *Black Beauty* activity on pages 23–28 by Jennifer Naraki. Used with permission. Photographs of the *Charlotte's Web* activity on pages 29–35 by Jennifer Pepito. Used with permission. Photographs of the *Crossover* activity on pages 36–43 by Kayla Smith. Used with permission. Photographs of the *Esperanza Rising* activity on pages 44–51 by Naomi Ovando. Used with permission. Photographs of the *Evolution of Calpurnia Tate* activity on pages 52–57 by Hannah Mayo. Used with permission. Photographs for the "Mother-Daughter Book Club" essay on pages 58–61 by Ana Ohlandt. Used with permission. Photographs of the *Farmer Boy* activity on pages 62–68 by Alison Blake. Used with permission. Photographs of the *From the Mixed-Up Files of Mrs. Basil E. Frankweiler* activity on pages 69–73 by Mandy Lackey. Used with permission. Photographs of the *Green Ember* activity on pages 75–79 by Hannah Mayo. Used with permission. Photographs of the *Heidi* activity on pages 80–83 by Ali Dover. Used with permission. Photographs of the *Hobbit* activity on pages 85, 89, and 90 by Mandy Lackey and on pages 86 and 87 by Alison Blake. Used with permission. Photographs of the *Island of the Blue Dolphins* activity on pages 92–97 by Hannah Mayo.

Used with permission. Photographs for the "Falling in Love with Authors" essay on pages 98–100 by Jennifer Dees. Used with permission. Photographs of the *Lion, the Witch and the Wardrobe* activity on pages 102–107 by Ali Dover. Used with permission. Photographs of the *Little House in the Big Woods* activity on pages 108–113 by Stephanie Beaty. Used with permission. Photographs of the *Little Princess* activity on pages 114–116 by Ali Dover. Used with permission. Photographs of the *Little Women* activity on pages 119–121 by Brianne Buskey. Used with permission. Photographs of the *Mrs. Frisby and the Rats of NIMH* activity on pages 123–128 by Raimie Harrison. Used with permission. Photographs of the *My Side of the Mountain* activity on pages 129–133 by Mandy Lackey. Used with permission. Photographs for the "Collaborating with Great Authors" essay on pages 134–136 by Sharon McKeeman. Used with permission. Photographs of the *Peter Pan* activity on pages 138–144 by Jennifer Naraki. Used with permission. Photographs of the *Pippi Longstocking* activity on pages 145–150 by Raimie Harrison. Used with permission. Photographs of the *Robin Hood* activity on pages 151–154 by Alison Blake. Used with permission. Photographs of the *Roll of Thunder, Hear My Cry* activity on pages 155–162 by Nicole Eliason. Used with permission. Photographs of the *Secret Garden* activity on pages 163, 165, and 167 by Mandy Lackey and on page 166 by Ali Dover. Used with permission. Photographs of the *Swiss Family Robinson* activity on pages 169–174 by Mandy Lackey. Used with permission. Photographs of the *Treasure Island* activity on pages 175–178 by Jennifer Naraki. Used with permission. Photographs of the *Vanderbeekers of 141st Street* activity on pages 179–182 by Keri Ann Swaim-Gamez. Used with permission.

Additional photography credits:

Page i: Amber O'Neal Johnston
Pages ii–iii: Sharon McKeeman
Pages iv–v: Raimie Harrison
Pages vi–vii: Jillian Ragsdale
Page 184: Nicole Eliason
Page 193: Rachel Kovac
Page 194: Raimie Harrison

Illustrations:

Recurring trees: pikolorante/Shutterstock
Page ix (gradient background): @jenteva/stock
.adobe.com
Page ix (book): @Tanya Syrytsyna/stock.adobe.com
Pages ix (three left stems with leaves), 47, 133, 157:
@moleskostudio/stock.adobe.com
Pages ix (right branch), 3 (nature images), 7 (leaves),
28 (trophy), 110, 111 (acorn), 118 (flowers), 124
(twig with berries), 139 (twig with leaves), 152
(leaf), 166, 168: @bloomicon/stock.adobe.com
Pages ix, 11, 17, 28, 30, 32–33, 37, 38, 41, 45, 51, 53,
63, 70, 76, 77, 81, 82, 83, 86, 93, 96, 115, 120, 124,
130, 139, 146, 152, 156, 164, 170, 176, 180 (small
watercolor stains): @irinabogomolova/stock
.adobe.com
Page 3 (book): @dariaustiugova/stock.adobe.com
Pages 5, 11, 53 (large watercolor stains):
@PureSolution/stock.adobe.com
Pages 5, 8 (cookie), 65, 78: Graphic Box/Creative
Market
Pages 7, 77, 83 (twigs): @kateja/stock.adobe.com
Page 8 (hat), 128: @Oksana/stock.adobe.com
Page 8 (jam jar): @kamenuka/stock.adobe.com
Page 11 (bottom watercolor splash): @artant/stock
.adobe.com

Pages 12, 34 (cupcake), 116: @vaneeva/stock.adobe
.com
Pages 15, 21, 177 (color stroke): @Danussa/stock
.adobe.com
Pages 19, 20, 25, 164 (radish), 170 (pineapple):
@artinspiring/stock.adobe.com
Pages 22, 40, 41 (stopwatch): @cat_arch_angel
/stock.adobe.com
Pages 24, 56 (butterfly), 177 (ship), 178: © Gisela
Goppel
Pages 34 (paint splash), 101, 103, 109, 115 (paint
splash), 117, 146 (paint splash), 180 (paint
splash): @sakura art/stock.adobe.com
Page 46: @anna42f/stock.adobe.com
Pages 50 (scissors), 79 (paintbrush), 118 (crayons),
161 (scissors): Paper Sphinx/Creative Market
Pages 51 (avocado), 122, 131: @vasabii/stock.adobe
.com
Pages 55, 56 (squirrel, acorn), 144: Dainty Doll Art/
Creative Market
Pages 56 (leaves), 111 (pinecone), 160 (holly
branch): Corner Croft/Creative Market
Page 67 (candle): Marina Ermakova/Creative Market
Page 67 (popcorn): @rulizgi/stock.adobe.com
Page 67 (milk bottle): @nataliahubbert/stock.adobe
.com
Pages 74, 79 (paint palette): @Ilona/stock.adobe
.com
Pages 84, 94, 97: Maria B. Paints/Creative Market
Page 91: @Viktoriia Manuilova/stock.adobe.com
Page 95 (dolphin): @AS.Makarova/stock.adobe.com
Page 95 (otter): @Artmirei/stock.adobe.com
Page 121 (gloves, glasses): @madiwaso/stock.adobe
.com
Page 121 (paint brush): @Ann Lukashenko/stock
.adobe.com
Page 126: @時々雨 /stock.adobe.com
Page 172: YesFoxy/Creative Market